ABSINTHE

WORLD LITERATURE IN TRANSLATION

THROUGH GERMAN
Contemporary Literature in Translation

Selected and translated by: Lauren Beck, Elisabeth Fertig, Ivan Parra Garcia, Lena Grimm, Özlem Karuç, Michaela Kotziers, Elizabeth Sokol, Silke-Maria Weineck, Veronica Cook Williamson

27

ABSINTHE: World Literature in Translation published by the
Department of Comparative Literature at the University of Michigan.

ABSINTHE: World Literature in Translation receives the generous support
of the following schools, offices, and programs at the University of Michigan:
Rackham Graduate School, Office of the Vice Provost for Global and Engaged
Education, International Institute, and the College of Literature, Science, and
the Arts.

Typesetting and Design
William Kalvin, Delmas Typesetting. Ann Arbor, Michigan delmastype.com

ISBN: 978-1-60785-754-9
ISSN: 1543-8449

https://journals.publishing.umich.edu/absinthe/
Follow us on Twitter: @AbsintheJournal

ABSINTHE
World Literature in Translation

Dwayne Hayes
Founding Editor

Silke-Maria Weineck
Editor-in-Chief

Yopie Prins
Chair of Comparative Literature
at the University of Michigan
Publisher

Judith Gray
Administrator

Lauren Beck
Elisabeth Fertig
Ivan Parra Garcia
Lena Grimm
Özlem Karuç
Michaela Kotziers
Elizabeth Sokol
Veronica Cook Williamson
Editors

Amanda Kubic
Júlia Irion Martins
Karl Gaudyn
Managing Editors

Ali Bolcakan
Research Fellow

ABSINTHE 27

III. Radio Play

Acknowledgments

We are grateful to the Department of Comparative Literature and to the Department of Germanic Languages and Literatures for their generous support. We especially wish to thank Yopie Prins, publisher of *Absinthe* and chair of Comparative Literature, and Silke-Maria Weineck, editor-in-chief of *Absinthe* and co-editor of this issue. We express our deepest appreciation to all of the authors and the publishers who granted us the copyright to publish these texts and to the translators who devoted their time and expertise to bringing these works to a new audience.

We would also like to thank Alja Kooistra for copyediting this issue of *Absinthe* as well as Lauren Stachew, Jason Colman, and Sean Guynes at Michigan Publishing for their production of the issue.

Through German:
Contemporary Literature in Translation

The voices of so many countries echo through the selection of contemporary literature here: Germany, Austria, and Switzerland, but also Turkey, Moldova, England, Syria, Ghana, Romania, Ukraine, and Israel. Images of a movement that is never free recur: passports, border patrols, wars, sadness, awkward encounters, words that do not quite fit. While this issue of *Absinthe* has a distinct international flair, it is not, however, a selection of *Migrantenliteratur*, a category that fences in writers as foreign rather than German or Austrian or Swiss, that pretends that some are always at home and some belong only with an asterisk. Rather, the voices we have translated into English here are all integral to the German-speaking world and its representation, whether the authors were born there, arrived decades ago, or came recently to perhaps find another home, perhaps pass through.

All of the authors are alive, but that may be the only thing they have in common. Not even all of the texts here were originally written in German: Abdullah Alqaseer's gutting story, "A Lie Named Germany," was written in Arabic before Mustafa Al-Slaiman translated it into German; Serhiy Zhadan's poems, translated into German by Claudia Dathe, originally appeared in Ukrainian. You will have heard of some of the authors; the names of others will likely be unfamiliar. Taken together, we believe that they give a fuller version of what it means to live in the Germanosphere in the twenty-first century, at a time when many Americans in particular still associate Central Europe with ethnically homogenous countries and its literature predominantly with white men.

All texts were chosen, translated, and collaboratively edited by a group of graduate students in the Departments of Comparative Literature, English, and Germanic Languages and Literatures at the University of Michigan: Lauren Beck, Elisabeth Fertig, Ivan Parra Garcia, Lena Grimm, Özlem Karuç, Michaela Kotziers, Elizabeth

Sokol, and Veronica Cook Williamson. Silke-Maria Weineck served as the faculty advisor and editor-in-chief.

We have decided to call this issue "Through German," a title that stresses the language as medium, passage, barrier, portal, or sieve. Translation itself is a common theme: translating your name or your identity, translating your cat, translating yourself into an older or a younger version of yourself, translating your identity, your childhood, your history, or seeing language merge with the natural world where meaning dissolves into materiality. It is only fitting, then, that the issue closes with a reflection on the very process of translation that the last text in this volume, Elfriede Jelinek's "Ballad of Three Important Men and Also of the Circle of Persons Around Them."

I. Poetry

Ronya Othmann

toss the little snapdragons behind you | that nothing fits with | from the natural history museum i know | you lie on thin sheets as on paper | a doe hounded into snow

Translated by Michaela Kotziers

[toss the little snapdragons behind you]

toss the little snapdragons behind you. you
must not turn around. leave everything
behind that reminds you of her. the
rubbish before the gate, you will spell that
in winter, as a sparrow spells march.
you already forgot what it was.
snow, as if it had never been here.
empty courtyard entries, a false
claim, the black-eyed susan
behind your back. no name for
your girl. the village has no home for
you. you can't even live
in the woods. you ask yourself, while you
go, if it is the pavement that cannot
carry your shoes, or your shoes
not the pavement.

[that nothing fits with]

that nothing fits with what i can
write under january. her hair on
my pillow still not enough for a
wig. i wish for hospital
beds like ships. white sheets, i give
everything away. arms, legs, torso, ovaries.
twilight is settling, drop for drop.
her hands are not the ones that
twist and turn me. i search the blue
for signs. under my
closed eyes. steps, her jacket
flapping around the hips, a knock on
wood, the door. it is not the time for
geraniums.

[from the natural history museum i know]

from the natural history museum i know:
if i grind sand between my
fingers, soil and coal, the vines
unrobe, the boar is riled up, rises up,
trims surrounding time. how are these
trees to be understood. and do the
hairs on my body count as a meadow. it's simplest to love
backwards. if while singing you join
a bird, you can do without the
whistling sound. from the natural history
museum i do not know: is that my
forest or yours. and a recoil that
grows in the grasses, like a
racket, gray in an ash, a
reaper too, a searcher, a looker, a
cause for. where to with the scab.

[you lie on thin sheets as on paper]

you lie on thin sheets as on
paper, a fluttering moth, a
delicate animal. i push your arms and
legs aside, their weight and you into
sleep. more cannot be staked out
by this field and to what ends. before
the house there stands rain and i in shoes.
how does a stranded doe act.
and now. only barley and crops wherever
you go. pin room, my
pinned hem is wet. and the place to wait
a piece of floor, a light speck, will
soon be its surrounding. i go though
bittersweetly. one must push something
in between like straw, that
muffles the step. you cannot read into
the spores. i linger in the
herbarium.

[a doe hounded into snow]

A doe hounded into snow, toward the vanishing point. as if
    everything were only a
sketch. the spruces have cleared. wherever you look, fieldwork.
i do not have another, only this plowing up, drudging around,
furrowing about. before it is flush with the white. // i follow no one
    only the
thawing, this trickling, tumbling. so much is evident. who sketched
    these maps
and drew these lines. you attempt yourself a little, take
as your example the high neck coats, the bleached hair. //
like an animal that licks its wounds, and i by a sea. but
here is only corrugated steel. a reverberation from afar, the highway
washes up all kinds of flotsam and me, with eyes closed // take
me to the land of my forefathers and a walking stick, so that
if needed, i can still defend myself in the grave.

Zafer Şenocak

Forgotten Journeys to the Past

I breathed by you | password world | at night every trip leads abroad | I could have stopped | Refugees run across the meadow

Translated by Özlem Karuç

Field Trip

Translated by Veronica Cook Williamson

I breathed by you
and the room suddenly became wide
windows in front of my chest
the eyes shut and in flight
houses dangled below me
on their ties
and one room became two
two words four
then strife endless time
and trembling walls
one person borders on the other
civilian life a continuation of war
by other means
how many words are four by four meters
I calculated in my head
and unlearned to divide
the door goes there
the window over there
and a little more wind please
onto the skin

password world
owner certificates for curbsides
houses open and lock themselves
passersby on the outskirts
on leave
fall over
roaring living
by the recreation area
city falcons bred and released
land on the windowsill
and the gutter across

at night every trip leads abroad
an old man and a young woman
two languages
which moves away
which returns home
no word uttered on the way
picture stories drive through the head
the night train
from the last century
been on the run
human beings driven into pits
and back again
under the heaven of the poor
the train is on time
at every border
foreign lands turn into foreigners
one speaks the other language
who are you when you are among them
an old man a young woman
time without train stations would be the longest river
On its route
Unsecured roundish objects made of glass
Above the heads could shatter

I could have stopped understanding everyone

I could have stopped thinking of tea at noon

I could have stopped, in my room, thinking of the eggshells in the
    kitchen, their filling assisting the dough in the oven towards a
    new skin color

I shouldn't have forgotten that an official petition must be
    submitted for every change of skin color, which must be
    approved

I should have smelled deadlines without thinking of them

I could not have known that the formulation of an application was
    a morning prayer

I should have heard the Father calling to prayer

I should have given up idolizing sleep in my youthful negligence

I should have written down all my laziness and my sins no longer to
    be remembered

I should have known that by forgetting my house forfeits space and
    the only room I have left measures hardly more than a coffin

I could have stopped

I shouldn't have been allowed to forget

I should have known

How it works

To repent without begging for guilt

Refugees run across the meadow in front of the school
Straightening the kinked flower stems
They do not want to be confused with truants
With the last dilettante escape of the captured
       Stop Halt!
don't you notice that we want to ride along

Between the berry bushes red and blue
Their stride assimilated they dare
To go up to the vineyards
       there the wood grouse pushed its call
       into the morning breath
between the full branches ripe and round
daylight has broken

Field Trip

the first hour begins before the blank blackboard
an indefinite article settles on the hatstand by the door
which head flies towards us
you grow up, suddenly
is the cross on the wall empty the one on which Jesus hung for
    years
he must have been removed overnight
or have taken an express train to Athens with a through coach to
    the Adriatic
just like the whole class did on a bitterly cold morning in early
    summer
in our pointless summer coats we stood on the hill of the Acropolis
    two nights later
and clawed Greek skills out of each other's eyes
none of us made it to Peloponnes
but to Hades in two nights

the history teacher did not want to be called Orpheus
his recollection did not reach that far
yet neither his name nor his face could conceal
his kinship to an Anatolian slave
it could have been worse for him
we had a wide range of names we traded with great élan
they leapt into the air and snapped indiscriminately like caged wild
    animals
grade eleven A lined up amounts to a cage
nobody arrived at the idea of release
the black panther gets in Orpheus' way
and rewrites history
you don't need memory for that
the fragment of a dream and a life begun just yesterday are enough
to tell a story[1]

---

[1]*Geschichte* in German could be translated as story or history.

the history teacher points to the blackboard on which the future
changes into physics
the physicist turns around he barely wants to name his formula
the one that entitles him to displace the history teacher
verse appears on the board
a text to sing along to
we intone it and the teacher covers his ears
even though he is praised for his deafness
hysterically he shouts at us we remain lyrical
the day transforms into a life's history
any life it is not yet a discipline we will never be old
to whom after all can you entrust your life at seventeen
I envy the half-orphans who grow up with the mother
the smell of feminine hands across the face at all times
then the flesh gets its money's worth
I imagine that biology is always feminine
and geography mixed-gender hybrid
in competition with algebra a small crooked
weeping willow in the schoolyard unimaginable what went on here
    back then
thirty-one years subtracted from
nineteen hundred seventy-five
the penal colony was housed here and the discipline at the time
geology
exhumations so no one can hide under his ancestors' gravestone
a starry sky tipped into the open pit Peace Plaza
their tongues fall out of the stones when you tip them over
silence is cement
the history teacher practices forgetting with us
who would not call him Orpheus
we knit summer coats out of transparent yarn
what risk we take in geography
for one day for the fraction of one day
we want to dig dig dig a tunnel
heading home a night train full of eleventh grade in an expedition
    coma
we crossed under state borders fell overboard

were reborn through open windows
in the wind's fluttering howl
then the train stopped
silence on command
bleary-eyed in lockstep
in the baggage fake marble souvenirs
splintered footprints from some coast
there we stood in rank and file
little green men wanted to see our passports
they were our own watching
over the country that was left for us

Serhiy Zhadan

The Rhinoceros |
The Cellist

Translated from Ukrainian to German
by Claudia Dathe

Translated from German to English
by Elizabeth Sokol

The Rhinoceros

For half a year she remains brave.
For half a year she gazes at death
like a rhino in the zoo —
dark wrinkles,
heavy breathing.
She is fearful, but she looks on,
she does not close her eyes.

Bad, truly bad.
It cannot be otherwise.
Death is bad, it creates fear.
It is bad to breathe the stench of the red moon.
It is bad to see how history arises.

Half a year ago everything was completely different.
Half a year ago everyone was different.
Nobody was frightened by the stars
that fell in the reservoirs.
Nobody was terrified by the fumes,
that rose from the cracks in the black floor.

In the middle of the nightly street,
between noise and fire,
between death and love,
she digs her face into his shoulder,
thrashes him with desperate fists,
cries and screams in the dark.
I don't want to see any of this, she says,
I cannot schlep all this around with me.
What's all the death to me?
How do I start with it?

How do you start with death?
Carry death on your back,
like a gypsy child

who is not loved by anyone
and does not love anyone?
Love is so scarce,
love is so defenseless.

Weep and partition the dark with your warm hands.
Weep and do not with one step leave his side.
The world will never be as it was.
We will not allow it
to be as it was.

Fewer and fewer bright windows on the empty street.
Fewer and fewer carefree passers-by
in front of the shops' displays.
In the diabolical autumn fog, fields and rivers grow cold.
The fires go out in the rain.
At night the cities die of frost.

The Cellist

The cellist drags
his wooden instrument,
stands still,
takes a breath,
barely holds himself up,
drags his legs
across the stony pavement.
How they just yell
in his face,
how they angrily pursue him,
surround him,
hurl curses at him.

Men run together,
women stand annoyed,
children throw pavement lemons
made of gold.

How many bitter words
he has heard in his life.
As if it were his fault
that he has to drag this devil's music,
his fault that he
cannot cast it off
in the middle of the street.
But whom can you make grasp this,
to whom can you explain it?
Screams tear the air,
Soon blood runs,
soon tears roll.

The men frown,
the women make noise,
the children imprint the sky into their memory

until the end
of their long days.

When they then leave
the city, stop on
the hill, he puts
his instrument on the ground,
takes the bow,
bends over the varnished wood,
grows one with it,
cannot tear himself away,
the movements are difficult,
on the battered palms of his hands,
blood congeals.
Then

the men weep,
the hearts of the women wilt,
the children wonder when
pearls
of musical hearing
grow in their fists.

II. Short Prose and Stories

Abdullah Alqaseer

A Lie Named Germany

*Translated from Arabic to German
by Mustafa Al-Slaiman*

*Translated from German to English
by Veronica Cook Williamson*

She has changed. Oumaimah's gaze is not as alert as before. Some-times she does not even notice what it is that moves her ten-year-old son, Farid, as if she were indifferent to it. Perhaps that is due to how constantly she had worried about her family in Syria, to all the tears shed and the perpetual prayers asking that the hail of bombs finally stop. Perhaps it is because she had steadily hoped to save her loved ones from death, the death that ravaged the region from which she came from in all directions.

Now she had arrived in a safe place, she thought, a place where she could finally find peace and have no need to worry about her child anymore. Yet this peace did not set in: she missed Amer, her husband, and her daughter, Ayah, too much. So she was often absentminded and pictured in her mind the longed-for reunion with the whole family after the long separation. If she was confronted with reality, however, she wept heartrendingly and spoke to those absent as if they were with her; she asked her husband and daughter how they had been faring since she and Farid had set off on their journey and when they would finally be on their way.

—Is that Germany, Mama?

—Yeah, Farid, that is Germany. We are in Germany now. Don't you like it here?

—Yes, I do, but I have a feeling that it is not the way that people described it to us in Syria. Whatever. The main thing is we finally do not hear bombs, cannons, or missiles anymore.

The words of the child weighed like boulders on Oumaimah's ears. How could she lie to her own child like that? Why had she not realized that the truth would come to light one day and that bad things would follow?

—Dear God! Don't they say that paradise lies at the feet of the mother? For all I care, you can throw me in Hell, but please, please turn this place into the Germany that they told us about. Are you not the sublime and the almighty!

One year had passed since the separation of Oumaimah's fam-ily. On the last evening they spent sitting together as a family, they were united foremost by the candle light and the dream of Germany. Farid, of course, could not care less about German human or animal rights; he could also do without his father's long-winded lectures on the economically advanced Germany, the social system, the unemployment benefits, and refugee relief. He was far more interested in his mother's promises that he would get a room full of toys once they arrived in Auntie Merkel's country—as they called it then. On the condition that he, on the long journey to her—from Syria through Turkey, with the death boats to Greece, then all the way into the land of dreams—stayed nicely patient.

—Mama, didn't papa always say that the most important thing is to learn German really fast?

—Yes, that's right, son. The language . . .

— . . . is the key to the country, he always said.

—Yes, exactly, son. (She laughed.)

—But Mama, then why does nobody here speak German?

Oumaimah went pale and her throat went dry.

—You're right, my son. We have so far only met people who are just like us. Be patient! We all need to be patient.

—But why? I want to play with German kids. I want to tell them about the airplanes, about the MiGs and F-16s. Do you know if they have such airplanes too?

—They definitely also have such planes, but they don't see them as often as we do.

—I want to tell them that my sister was so scared (with that he spread his arms and eyes wide open) when she saw the amputated leg of our neighbor Aby Ibrahim lying on the street.

—You'd better not do that, you'll only scare them with such terrible stories.

—But what else should I tell them about?

—Farid, sweetie, as long as you don't speak German, they won't understand you anyway.

With each of the child's questions, the mother's lie grew, along with her worry, how to ever find her way out of this lattice of lies. That she had lied to her son lay heavy on her, and she constantly feared that the moment of truth had arrived. Repeatedly she tried to tell him the truth, but she never had the heart to do it. Then she thought again, time will fix everything and it is better this way.

Her sole distraction was those who newly arrived from Syria. She hurried to them again and again in order to look for her husband and daughter. But once again the two were not among the refugees. Suddenly she recognized a woman in the mass of people: it was her neighbor Um Saraj, the tailor. She ran to her, hugged her, asked about her journey—which route she took and how the journey had been. But Um Saraj was curt and merely answered, "I was led here by what led you here too. I took the route that you took too. Be patient, they who have not come, will still come." And she went on.

Oumaimah stopped dead in her tracks. She laid a hand on her chest. Then she heard a voice from farther away, "Oumaimah, Oumaimah!" She turned towards the sound of the voice and saw him: Amer. Actually Amer! At first, she did not trust her eyes. Then she was overcome by a feeling as if someone were pulling a too-tight sweater off her, with her head getting stuck. But strong like a bull-fighter, she leaped towards him, when suddenly her daughter Ayah's face appeared in her mind. She held his face in her hands and cried out, "Where's Ayah? Did Ayah not come with you? Where is she?" He closed his eyes, lowered his head, and said:

—Ayah stayed behind. Ayah's still alive.

—What? Who did you leave her with?

—I don't know. I can't remember anymore. When the barrel bombs fell, I grabbed her and ran. Her legs were broken, and her face was smeared with blood. She was screaming her head off. The paramedics took her from me and brought her to the hospital. I was only slightly injured. I went back to help the others, who were lying under the rubble. But there was nothing we could do, for another barrel bomb fell, and it brought me here.

Silent tears ran down Oumaimah's cheeks as she heard Amer's words. She relentlessly kissed her husband, soaking his shoulders with her tears. They remained intertwined until they caught sight of Farid behind them.

—Mama, I knew that we weren't in Germany.

—Farid, sweetie!

—Are you not afraid of God, mama? Do you want to go to hell and leave me behind, all alone? Is this paradise, papa? In paradise, are there only us, our neighbors, and children from our neighborhood?

—Farid, you were asleep when we . . .

—When I died, right? Why haven't we seen God yet, mama? We've been here so long already. Does God not care?

—Farid, calm down, please.

—I'll demand that God teach me German. I'll tell him about the MiGs and the F-16s. I'll ask him if he, too, has such airplanes. I'll tell him about my sister's fear when she saw our neighbor's amputated legs on the street. And about my sister's broken legs and the blood on her face, about the ambulances, the barrel bombs, and the place where my sister is now. I promise you, I'll tell him everything.

Farid moved away from his parents and disappeared into a mass of children until he could not be seen anymore. And the faces of the children formed a cloud that rose into the sky until it rained tears.

Catalin Dorian Florescu

The Navel of the World

Translated by Lena Grimm

Father crosses himself and says, "We got lucky."

Father often dreams of Grandfather and how he comes towards him, straight through walls. Sometimes he appears so suddenly that my father wakes up sweaty and afraid. On days like those, my father insists, he will receive bad news.

On days like those, the letters remain lying on the hallway floor, and he peers at them only from a distance. One day later, Grandfather or not, they are opened, as if the contents were now different than the day before. Father has this quirk about superstitions. When he talks like that, the farmer's son in him comes back to life, and with the farmer's son, the other villagers too, living and dead, the wide, dry plain of the Danube, the animal herds, and the sun of his childhood. But more than anything, the superstitions as well, and with them droves of vampires, witches, ghosts, and the undead. "There was not a Christian soul in the street after sunset," he says. "Vampire hour. Everyone in their houses and Dracula on the streets." Father exaggerates occasionally.

Dracula was the one with long teeth who instilled fear in voluptuous Victorian women. He left Transylvania when it became too boring for him there. Dracula was the first emigrant from my home. In 1982, we followed—Father, Mother, and I—but you don't need to be afraid: we're not directly related.

"We got lucky," says Father and exhales loudly, in order to demonstrate his relief. "We took the last train," says Mother and looks mournful. After Father has made the sign of the cross, he turns the radio on. Radio Free Europe. The same station for eighteen years, every day at six o'clock. Father listens to home. When I'm visiting, I listen with him. Then I'm little again, tiny, and I see the both of us at home. At home on the street with the train station, where trains were still real trains, with fuming locomotives, groaning noises, and so on. Where there was no reason to be nostalgic, because nostalgia simply wasn't part of the plan. Nostalgia is the price that only gets added once you are stuck. In Switzerland, for example.

When Father and I listen to the radio, our eyes shine and we take turns saying "shh! shh!" whenever the other talks too loudly. Father has the best commentary—he even knows the voices from the radio by name. He knows the contexts. Because I like listening to him, I ask him about them. He likes to give answers and expands them into true stories. From my father, I inherited storytelling. From my mother, the graveness. Not too much, though, just enough to be grounded. You need to be grounded, if you don't want to float into the air like a weather balloon and fly homewards with all the voices from the radio.

On an August morning, 1982, everything became different than it was before. When I woke up, nothing in the apartment had changed. It was tidier than usual, since Mother had made a special effort; she didn't want anyone to think that she was a bad housewife after we left. Father had thought that her labor was pointless. By the time someone realized that we weren't coming back, the dust would have long settled again. Mother didn't let that unsettle her, and so we lived the last days at home as if in a museum. Only in the closets, the clothes were already missing, and little white slips of paper lay everywhere with the names of those who should get our things. I thought, "In this way, little pieces of us go everywhere."

If I made an effort, I would not even notice the slips of paper. Just don't look, go into the bathroom—a slip-free room—wash, change, and set out. We ate breakfast quickly and afterwards Mother wiped down the kitchen table, washed and dried the dishes, and placed them back in the cupboard. Father inspected the windows, the water faucets, the gas range, then was the last to leave the apartment. He locked the door twice, joined us in the elevator, and so we went silently down eight floors. Later, everything would be distributed according to our wishes. In my imagination, however, everything still lies in its place, even today, complete with white slips of paper. Not even the dust has settled. It is still and shady.

I can no longer remember if I regretted our departure or if I wished for it. If I was afraid. If I chose myself. It was a sequence of events, nothing more, and in this instance, memory fails. Maybe it was even a little bit exciting. Me, a little fellow traveler.

Switzerland fell in our laps like a lottery prize. Father had a good nose for this sort of thing. In front of a modest hotel in Zürich, after many days of travel through Europe, and ready for further travel,

Father asked a fine gentleman on the street for advice. Thirty seconds of inspiration was enough to overcome despair. It was like a soccer game when all is settled with a goal in the ninetieth minute. Whether the fine gentleman was God, we don't know. The only thing that we remember is that he drove a dark limousine.

To be clear: we stayed in this place because someone—God, for example—wrote down the name of someone who helped us further. Within seconds it was a done deal. One spends years making plans, but the crucial things happen quick as lightning. It could have been Patagonia. That it ended up being Switzerland, though, makes us especially happy even today. "The navel of the world, boy," Father says, "the navel of the world. We got lucky." Lottery home. We didn't dare to think that it could be Switzerland. Switzerland was closer to a plaything of the imagination. One day you stand smack in the middle of it, possibly meet God, and eighteen years later, you're surprised at how much time has passed.

Today, Father watches Africa on the TV and records animal films on video. When hunting scenes are shown and the lionesses prowl in the high savanna grass, he calls us all together. This is almost as nice as listening to our home language on the radio together. Sometimes a gnu even survives.

Father rewinds the film in order to check that the recording is alright. Then the lioness chases after the gnu all over again, and the gnu gets a second chance. But it dies just as pitifully as the time before. Father presses the pause button as the animal falls to its knees. He labels the tape and says, "I know a video in which the gnu makes it. It just pretends to be dead and runs away as soon as the lioness isn't paying attention. Gnu-cunning."

In Father's video collection, gnus die, aliens land, Lady Di has an accident, and a tremendous number of goals are scored. But the most common are reports from home. Short segments, often just the last few minutes. But in order to recognize home, one doesn't need more than a few seconds. Even before one word is spoken, something catches the eye, and breath comes faster. The essence is visible then.

The particular kind of interior in a farmer's house, for example. Tapestry, woodstove, embroidered tablecloth, image of Jesus. Thick bedspreads and pillows in the background. The farmer woman's dress: durable material, because of the hard work, flower pattern on the skirt, headscarf. A shrug, a nod, a smile. The courtyard with the draw well and the horse-drawn cart for the daily drive to the field. Behind it, the village pub: one room, three tables, five drunks. Barely any choice on the menu: schnapps in dark and light bottles. Intoxication takes care of itself. Chocolate Brand East, hard and bitter.

Then the TV camera enters another courtyard. There, they celebrate a wedding. The bride dances with her father and cries. The groom empties a glass of schnapps in one go. The dress rehearsal for the daily trip to the pub later. But such details don't interest us. We sit as if bewitched until the film is at its end. Afterwards, Father inspects the quality of the recording. Like with the gnus.

We were good emigrants from the beginning. Assimilated to the customs, white, and completely European besides that too. Lucky. People don't see our foreignness. Most, at best, hear it. Rolling Rs, the wrong word order, the wrong articles, the wrong case, long rows of "ums" until the right word comes to mind, helpful use of the word "thingamajig" or the question "how do you say that again?" always a bit effusive in tone. But the Swiss don't hold something like that against us, some even love the rolling Rs.

The problem is you don't want to stand out yourself. Standing out, not belonging. A permanent stay in a foreign zone. Illegality in perpetuity. For eighteen years already.

The pauses for thought have waned, words arrive more quickly on the tongue, and one is taken as someone "from here" more often. Okay, not exactly "from here," but less and less often "from there." From the mountains, for example. From areas where the Swiss also roll their Rs. For our sake, add in something soft, something good for emigrant tongues, for Father's tongue, for example.

Father says, "These tongue twisters put my brain in a twist." Even though he could be content. Our language here—finally I say "our"—is soft in general. Almost no strong language. So you could flat-out disregard the tongue twisters. So you could be literally happy to get by without any force at all. At any rate, no more force than is necessary to stay put. After eighteen years, I still arrange the words in my mouth like pearls I am about to spit out. When I'm insecure, I mumble and imagine that no one notices.

You say "I love you" and feel nothing. You say "I hate you" and feel nothing. You only feel something once you translate it inside. Into the language of your childhood. Into the language in which Father cursed and the first girl desired me. If you still feel nothing, even then, you're lost.

Refugee passport. Blue with two gray stripes in the top right corner. If you have a passport like this, or another one with the wrong colors, the problems already start at the consulate.

"Foreign ID, work verification, confirmation certificate for health insurance. Confirmation certificate of a room reservation for the entirety of your stay, otherwise a declaration by the guest family to be acquired at city hall and signed by them concerning the defrayal of all additional costs during your stay in France. Hospital, property damage in case of accidents, and so on. A current bank statement. A month's waiting time, maybe shorter. What? You still have questions? I can't answer that, Monsieur. Please step aside. Next person, please. No, Monsieur, procure the documents checked on the form and then come again. Take a number on the ground floor and wait until you are called. Excuse me? Two photos, Monsieur, not four. Excuse me? Yes, 80 Francs for a one-time visa. Now step aside, Monsieur, you're standing in the way. What do you mean? Why don't I raise my head when I answer you? Please step aside, Monsieur."

I asked the Madame at the counter if she didn't want to know my dick size too. Maybe it was important, for France. Asked complete with rolling Rs and in French. She raised her head and balked, "Excuse me, Monsieur?" Stay polite, Madame. By any means, stay polite. I had barely asked the question when all of the other people waiting were laughing already. In the house of the French consulate in Zürich, liberating laughter spread. Anyone who understood even just a little bit of French was laughing.

They threw me out and locked the heavy door behind me. I kicked it. The door opened again, just a crack, and a bald man appeared. He said, "I will remember you, Monsieur. You won't receive a visa for France now, Monsieur. No decency, Monsieur."

"Who has no decency here?" I retorted, and saw everyone behind him, who had laughed before, duck their heads. "Chauvinists!" I yelled, "all hairless and chauvinistic!" It is useful to know that baldness and nationalism are linguistically close in France: chauve, chauvin.

In the middle of Zürich, then, I hit a border, hidden out of sight on the second story of an unremarkable house. You go about and believe yourself to be free, and suddenly freedom is no longer there. Suddenly it hurts, and you're foaming with anger.

I live here happily. It is not an excessive happiness. It is the happiness of having a dependable lover. Slightly pedantic, slightly boring, slightly flexible. You are used to her bad breath. You save up the sex for someone else. For later, when real life begins. But, when exactly does real life start? And what kinds of decisions need to be made for it to happen?

Father is content here. "The Swiss were our salvation," he says, and then lists everything from which we were saved. And yet my father has longings. Do you know how I recognize it? From six o'clock news on the radio. From Father's attentiveness, his careful listening. From his recall, which doesn't skip a single program. I recognize it by the way he curses home only to return there each year. He's on his way again right now. Now he has a cell phone with him, so that he can maintain a connection. He stopped and called near the border between Hungary and Romania. Who would have thought that one day you could calmly step out of your car, exhale, and call your son. Back then, there was only one thing to do near the border: be afraid and piss your pants.

This particular sensitivity to borders. As places at which one appears, in person, and with a broad back for the rubber clubs. Where one can no longer say, "I'll be fine. I am just one of many." Where pissing your pants is one of the last remaining freedoms. A gnu without a second chance.

Men in uniform say, "Come with us." Men in uniform take the whole car apart. Men in uniform make other men undress themselves. Behind the steering wheel, I shrink into a small boy who wants to close his eyes and imagine himself elsewhere. Or pretend to be dead. That would be something.

The emigrant has it just as bad as the unlucky daughter in the fairy tales. At first glance, she is plain and cast out. Until she finds her prince and transforms herself, one has to read many pages. With the emigrant, no one knows exactly how many pages there are until the transformation occurs and he will be free of fear.

In the meantime, the task is to be brave and to say it out loud just once: "My land." "My land" for eighteen years already. I have been asked about my land many times while abroad. I rarely knew an answer. Temporary answers. Something like answers in development. But I will practice giving answers. I will definitely do that.

I stand in the midst of life, in the midst of myself, and thirty-three is a good age. Thirty-three is surely a good age for something.

Marina Frenk

long ago and not really true

Translated by Lauren Beck

24

(Berlin, Germany, now)

I'm too petty for suicide, that would be bordering on pathos, like my shitty pictures. Besides, Karl needs me. I am stuck in my daily life, in my comparative affluence. If I still lived in Eastern Europe and weren't some oligarch's daughter, which of course I'm not, I would think of myself as rich. What would I actually do if I still lived in Moldova, or in Romania, Latvia . . . someplace I've apparently never been? I've dabbed my burns with disinfectant. Now I inspect the skin, which seems to be puckering up, and imagine the cells invisibly trying to regenerate. I throw myself onto the bed that Marc hasn't slept in for ages and push the pillow tightly against my face. I push it down into my memory: I was in my early twenties when I flew to Chişinău, alone for the first time. I exited the airplane, and on the bus to the terminal looked at the other people, many of whom gave off the impression that arriving in their home country was a national holiday; they seemed proud and relaxed, and in a way, I admired them, because I felt nothing, just the same otherness as everywhere else. I stood in the main hall and had forgotten that Moldova does not belong to the EU. "This country is not in the European Union," rang in my head. It burned, it almost boomed. I kept moving ahead in the line to passport control and began to pray: "The EU solves economic problems. The EU creates free trade areas in accordance with the will of the EU itself, which serve the long-term stabilization of the country. The EU is the country's main trade partner for the country. Why does the EU do that? Does it have too big a heart? Because that is how it receives money from Moldova, by selling crap from the EU in the marketplace in Moldova."

Reflexively, I pull the pillow off my head and gasp for air. My parents often prophesied before that if I still lived in Eastern Europe, I would sell crap from China in the marketplace or wash dishes somewhere. See, some people can see into the future, my parents can see a non-existent present by means of a non-occurred past. Obviously the other way around is better—rather buy crap from China here in the discount shops than sell it there in the market-place. . . . But I would probably do the exact same thing in Moldova that I do in Germany: vomit onto my canvas and pretend that it's art. How do you say "пошлость" in German, I wonder and stuff a corner of the pillow into my mouth, can't breathe, and spit it back out, coughing. There is no translation. Banality, platitude, obscenity. But none of those describes the same thing that the word "пошлость" does in Russian . . . it means much more than banal or lewd or slimy or crude, it describes my soul and my paintings. This word's meaning, "poshlost," it smells like putrid meat, tastes like wet cigarettes, looks morally reprehensible if you're moral. Its meaning can only be understood if in some regard you are still moral, because when all memories of any values are truly extinct, "poshlost" reigns, and what that is cannot be translated into German. Impossible. I press the pillow against my face again and try to endure not breathing; maybe this is how I'll finally learn to dive as well.

I stood in the line for passport control at the airport and feared its end. I decided to laugh off the whole situation and imagined that I am not me, I was always good at that. I could transform myself because I got lost at the beach as a kid once. As a precaution, I prayed my post-Soviet prayer all the way through to the end: "The EU is the country's main trade partner because it sells its crap in the marketplace in Moldova, so my parents were right, someone is always selling crap in the marketplace. Russia says: if you don't cooperate with the EU, we won't buy your wine, nyah-nyah! But Moldova only sells wine. Russia weakens the Moldovan economy: if you cozy up to Europe, we won't buy your wine, nyah-nyah! When it comes to the Moldovans themselves, one half wants the EU to be their momma, and the other half wants the Eurasian Economic Union." I learned this designation by heart in case someone should ask . . . does Moldova really want to be independent?

The EU solves economic problems. The EU creates free trade areas, I think and chew on the corner of the pillow.

"Identification!" a smoky mechanical voice demands from me. A robot that smokes?

"No, I don't have my passport on me, just my ID card," I apologize.

"Were you born in Chişinău?" asks another voice, female, not smoky, but judgmental.

"Yes, I was." Smirks. Whispers. Snickers. "And why did you give up your citizenship?"

"Because I'm an AIWN."

"A what?"

"Absolute Idiot Without a Nationality."

"What??"

"Mother's Russian, father's Jewish," I say, crossing my eyes. A contemptuous glance on her part. Whispers. Phone call. Marching off. Searching.

I spent one night at the airport and flew back again. I returned a few months later, this time with a passport and the understanding that Moldova was really something different from the better Europe. It is to this day, and at some point, it will probably just be Russia again, just like it was the Soviet Union for a long time, because it is too small for its own independence.

I crawl into bed with my head under the pillow and cry bitterly. What's the point of this senseless blubbering? Why can't I function? I don't feel desired anymore, loved anymore, seen anymore, I don't see anything anymore myself, except the subject of this strange painting I finished over the past weeks that I myself call "poshlost." I'll put it up with the other paintings in the attic since I have no gallerist, no agent, no photos of my success on Facebook. Not anymore, I died over those last few years. I sweat under the pillow, my nose runs, my tears turn the pillowcase and the sheets all wet and slimy, and I would love to dive deep underwater, which I don't dare to do. I want to dive into the depths of our origin to look at the algae and fish and water bugs, to shiver naked in the icy water and to just open my mouth in order to try to become an organism capable of letting liquid into its lungs. To adopt this glassy fish gaze from that Catherine of my dream and to drift through the water as if in slow motion while I occasionally let my mouth gape open to swallow smaller fish. *"A fish doesn't think because a fish knows everything."*

I close my eyes, do not breathe, and observe my fear. Marc's inner abyss is as dark as it is here with my eyes closed under my pillow. Darkness that is darker than it can be, blinder than blind. He does not talk about it.

I throw the pillow at the floor lamp and gasp for air. I stare at our bedroom ceiling. "What is depression?" I once asked him. "No more interest," he answered.

His fingers' tenderness transformed over time into an immobility made of viscous gel, enclosed by his thick skin that no longer lets anything through. He does not talk with me anymore.

Barbara Honigmann

Strasbourg, December 24th

Translated by Ivan Parra Garcia and Lauren Beck

My husband is called Peter, my sons are called Jo and Ru, and our cat is called Atze. Miss Atze.

Our street is a small street on the edge of downtown Strasbourg next to the new development called Esplanade. There is not one tree or one shrub in the street, and it is not at all quiet; rather, cars drive through perpetually, even if you don't know where to. Across from our house there is a France Télécom building, the ugliest building in all of Strasbourg, the second ugliest one being our house, but we don't notice it anymore, because we have been living here for so long. Our children grew up on this street, Jo has since moved out, Ru is rarely seen, and I have never lived in an apartment as long as in this one; sometimes, it is a little frightening, this duration.

1984 is when we moved here, we had come from East Berlin, and whenever we are asked why we didn't just move to West Berlin, we explain that we are a Jewish family and we were looking for a connection to a Jewish life that does not exist in Germany.

Beyond that we were simply looking for variation, a change, and maybe even a little bit of an adventure, and we found it, too, so much so that we are still exhausted today. Besides the adventure of the foreign language, it mainly consists of life between the countries, the worlds, the cultures, each of which we participate in on the margins. A difficult balancing act, in which you can easily fall between all stools.

The small sketches gathered here were originally columns written for the *Basler Zeitung*. They appeared there between 1991 and 1996 in supplement "3," the newspaper for the tri-state region on the Upper Rhine between France, Germany, and Switzerland. They are a bit of a chronicle of our life here, from the time when my sons changed from boys into young men. Today is December 24th, Christmas for most people on our street, but for us it is an ordinary day. For the Turkish man on the corner it is also an ordinary day. Just now I got milk and mineral water from him. An odd clientele had assembled there, non-Christians, marginals, and lonely hearts.

Barbara Honigmann

My Life as a Cat |
In the Golden Cage

Translated by Lauren Beck

My Life as a Cat

Summer is hardly a season—it rather resembles another life. It is not yet truly vacation time, since we only go to the sea in August, but this month of July no longer belongs to the working year either. The sky is far too blue, the sunshine seems exaggerated, the kids are all on summer break and just loaf around all day or go to "Phantasialand" with their day camp. The city feels deserted; at least here, in my neighborhood, around the university, everything has died down, and I feel abandoned, like a stranger in my own land.

All this leads to me not having any desire to go to my desk and to work, or at least to pretend to, for how often do I just do my time there, and nothing goes forward, and nothing goes backward either. Absolutely nothing comes to me. In any case, when summer breaks out, all effort feels pretty pointless to me, and my life approximates that of our striped cat. I would like to do nothing more than lie stretched out in the sun like her and when it gets too hot, curl up in the shade until the evening. Only late do we both get a bit friskier, she stops by at her food bowl and catches a couple of flies, and I could go out now and have an ice cream coffee on the terrace with Peter, but even there, we probably would not talk much, even though we usually have so much to discuss. My ambition has shattered, all my plans have evaporated. Write novels? What for? Paint pictures? In this heat? A book? Is there anything new under the sun? The cat thrives like this, after all, she has no plans and no ambition and pursues nothing but her flies and is nonetheless loved and the star of the family.

She lies there purring on my desk, stretched across books, binders, and papers, and will not let me get to work anyway. The pen in my hand is pawed away decisively. She is probably right. She must dream sometimes, and in my head it does not look any different now either, a couple of memories and fantasies are fluttering around. The cat licks her fur, and I will go take a shower now.

In the Golden Cage

Our cat named Atze is torn between whether she should remain lying in ambush fighting the snowflakes from under the cover of the laundry rack on the balcony or would rather roast her belly on her spot above the heater after all. I advise her to stay out on the balcony, for how often do we even get snow here anyway, it must have been three years now since we last saw snow on our street. And besides, I tell the cat, I will be going soon, and then I will close the door to the balcony again, and that will be it for your yard exercise this morning. For our cat is not allowed on the street below, because we're afraid that she will get run over or taken away, and because there are no trees or bushes or really anything resembling nature around there anyway, just concrete, asphalt, and cars. We call this decision prudent, what the cat calls it, we do not know. Thus, she lives in a golden cage, and her entire life from beginning to end takes place in our apartment, the view from the windows and the excursions onto the balcony are her only connections to the outside world. I often look at her and ask myself whether she is very unhappy about that and longs for the world behind the apartment door, which does sometimes stand open for a couple of minutes, after all. Of course, we provide her with news from outside, and not just in the form of food from cans and boxes, but rather, when we return from a trip, for instance, we leave our bags or suitcases standing around open and untouched for a couple of days, then she can thoroughly sniff after scents from the unknown and rummage through their innermost contents. We leave a lot of stuff lying around otherwise, too, which makes for cat-friendly territory as well, we have sacrificed all our blankets for cat sleeping spots. Peter built a climbing tree with a scratching post for her, and I brought a corner comber back for her from New York, and she really does use it to thoroughly comb her fur every day. This way, we might find mercy in front of a cat court. But now Atze has already had enough of the silly snowflakes and must, of course, see to it that she doesn't squander her eighteen hours of sleep. She pads over to me, looks at me, and clearly wants to say, "Man, your worries and Rothschild's money!"

Ronnith Neumann

Encounter by the Sea

Translated by Ivan Parra Garcia

I imagine:

I am a very old woman. I am happy, since I write books for children and live on an island, I live by the sea.

In my house's rooms, you can hear the buzzing of the cicadas, you can hear the waves come and go and ebb in the sand. My house stands on the edge of a high cliff facing the sun. It is not big, it is spacious and bright. Oleander blossoms in the garden, bougainvillea climbs up the walls, an olive tree shades the wooden furniture group where I sit and work in the mornings, at night jasmine scents the air.

From the veranda, you overlook the wide bay and the sea, the mysterious colors of the water, carefully graded, streaks of torn fields, flowing apart, lichen in blue-green, the white crests of the waves glitter. The veranda is entwined in vines, the heavy, dark grapes grow into my mouth. The village is a little farther up the street. The ornate little church rings in the morning, at noon, and in the evening.

On Sundays they celebrate their festivals.

I imagine:

I walk down the steep stairs, lined with pine and cypress trees, to the bay below the house. I walk slowly, but I am healthy and strong, and my legs are still willing, I am old and happy.

Up from the bay, the laughter of the vacationers rings towards me, the scent of sunscreen rises into my nose.

I imagine:

I meet a young girl in the bay below my house. The young girl and I: we sit opposite each other. We sit at a table on the terrace of a fish restaurant. All tables are occupied. The restaurant is named after the bay. It is a very small restaurant, it does not have a large selection of dishes, but it does have a good cook. He prepares the dishes according to ancient recipes that no one else knows anymore. Many come here from far away. The cook is known on the island. The tourists benefit from that. I have known the cook for many years.

The young girl opposite me is happy, since she writes stories for children, and she is taking a long and cheerful island vacation by the sea. She lives in a rented room above the bay, diagonally down from my house. She lives alone, but likes to live alone. She describes the room's interior. She describes it as simple, practical, and pretty. In the room next door lives a family with two children. The children are loud, but that does not bother her. She loves children. She speaks in an easy-going way, in short and clear sentences, without coyness. Her natural manner pleases me. I like to listen to her.

We both drink coffee. The people around us are noisy. A donkey screams in the distance. A dog yowls. Extended and hoarse.

I imagine:

The old woman treats the young girl to a piece of cake. The young girl is happy about it, she laughs, her laughter is clear and ringing. The old woman thinks: like the ringing of the bell up in the church tower. So bright and ringing. She enjoys her laugh. She likes the girl. She would like to hear her laugh even more.

They both drink a second cup of coffee. And eat the cake. A young couple play beach ball on the beach. Someone tries to start the motor of his inflatable boat.

I imagine:

The old woman invites the young girl up to her house. On the way, they stop by the girl's room. She fishes out a t-shirt and a pair of shorts from the dresser. The dresser is old and dusty just like the rest of the room. The room is dark but cool. The toilet is outside in the hallway. The plaster is peeling on the walls. The old woman does not like the room. She casually knows the landlady. The wall of the house is frail and rotten. There was an inspection once—years ago. But that is long forgotten. The landlady is taciturn and bitchy. No one can muster up the courage to speak to her. The girl has never seen her. She has rented the room through an agency.

She simply leaves the beach bag with the wet things on the floor. Hairpins are scattered all over.

I imagine:

The old woman and the girl sit on the veranda of the house. It is September, and the wine is ripe. The girl admires the grapes. A bunch of grapes lies heavily in her hand, full-blooded. She picked it herself. The girl's eyes shine. She exclaims: what a dream house, and this view, one can only dream about it, raves: oh! one day I . . .

The old woman remembers her dreams. The memory has pretty much faded. Above the mountain, the afternoon cloud drifts towards the valley.

I imagine:

The young girl talks about the disco down on the beach, about the boys and how pushy they are, their crude jokes, she talks about her boyfriend, in the city where she studies, and she stuffs her mouth with the grapes in her hand. Her eyes shine, brown crusts form around the laughing corners of the mouth.

When asked, she talks about the stories she writes, for the children, just like that. She looks around and asks. The old woman listens and smiles. Long extinguished memories befall her. All of a sudden. And like an attacking animal.

I imagine:

The young girl stays for dinner. The old woman finds sliced chicken, salad, and a dry country wine in the fridge. The young girl says: the wine is good, but dusty. They both have to laugh at that. The wine is cold and refreshing. They let it gurgle down their throats. For dessert they have figs in yogurt and honey. The figs are still warm from the tree. Tree-warm, the old woman says. The girl has never eaten fresh figs. Only those for Christmas. The dried ones. From the plates. At the end, they drink a mocha. The spoon will stick straight up in that, the girl says. But the handle of the spoon tilts to the edge. At that they both have to laugh. They sweeten the mocha with a liqueur.

From afar, the strange call of an early night bird sounds.

I imagine:

The old woman and the young girl stroll through the village. The young girl stops at the church. She admires the old frescoes, the rain-weathered facade. The church bells ring in the evening. They stand under the plane trees. The ringing of the bells and the laughter of the girl blend into a bright cheerful tone.

Inside the candles glow. Warm, cozy, and calm.

Only the crackle of the wicks fills the silence.

I imagine:

The villagers gaze at the girl, they follow her with their eyes. A pretty girl, they say, ask: your daughter? Granddaughter? The old woman smiles, shakes her head. She understands the words, the sentences. But only a few. She figures out the context herself.

She is esteemed. Here. She needs the security. The villagers timidly love her. Some know her books. Others know her from stories. The rest of them pretend to know her. The language of the children is international. Her language knows no borders.

I imagine:

The young girl likes it in the village. She likes the laughter of the old men and women, the sound of tossed-out words she does not understand. She stands in the shade of the plane trees on the plaza in front of the church and laughs with the men and the women.

The men pat her on the shoulders, the women take her in their arms, caress her hair. Above it all the plane trees whisper. The old woman takes the girl's arm. She feels the moist velvety coolness of her skin, the fine sweat-beaded hairs. The girl has never been in the village before. She hadn't gone that far up the mountain at all. The fine blonde hairs on her arm glitter over her tan.

I imagine:

The old woman breathes in the scent of the girl's arm. It smells of the salt of the sea, of old memories, long forgotten. The young girl laughs her laugh, her face above the old woman sinks down, towards her. The old woman senses the lips, strong, full lips and very gentle, in her hair. She closes her eyes, by her inner eye passes the red of the lips, full-blooded, and alive. A hint of beautiful fantasies.

The girl's hand, the long cool fingers stroke her cheek. The old woman feels a tear. She has never been so happy. The young girl erupts in laughter. One of the men planted a kiss on her cheek.

I imagine:

The old woman gazes after the girl in the dusk as she descends the stairs to the bay, lined with pine and cypress trees. The girl walks securely and quickly with easy, lively steps. She carries a plastic bag with figs and grapes in her hand. In the kitschy postcard view, the crescent moon adorns a nearby pine slope.

The old woman is a little afraid for the girl. She doesn't know why. She gazes after her. The memories have evaporated now. The girl waves, a small white hand disappears in the evening twilight.

It is getting dark. The darkness spreads. The southern night is quickly falling. From one minute to the next.

I imagine:
The old woman sits on the vine-entwined veranda of her house, the girl hunkers down in her dark rented room. Down in the bay the waves come and go, ebb in the sand. The nocturnal cicadas buzz their songs.

I imagine:
Both listen to the buzzing of the cicadas, the coming and going of the sea. To the ebbing. To time. Which drips away. Unrelenting. In the darkness of the room. Under the vine tendrils of the veranda.

I imagine:
The old woman in the house on the cliff, above the bay, that is me.
I imagine:
The young girl in the rented room above the bay yet beneath the old woman's house, that is me.
I imagine:
I am both. I am two.
I live in my own house. I live in a rented room.
I am a very old woman. I am a young girl. I am the middle of both. I am neither of them.
I imagine:
I have only encountered me. On the island. In the bay. Below, by the sea.

Sharon Dodua Otoo

The Story of Circle
and Quadrangle

Translated by Özlem Karuç

Once upon a time there was a circle that lived in a community of quadrangles. The circle spoke like the quadrangles and behaved like them. It was startling: it could even pretend to be a quadrangle whenever the situation called for it—which in fact happened very often. Sometimes it was enough for the circle to simply say nothing. Whenever the values of the quadrangles, such as being angular, were passionately held up high, short but clear lip service was advantageous. The circle always delivered that, in a well-behaved way, too, without wanting to contemplate much. Gradually, of course, the quadrangles stopped paying attention to the otherness of the circle. Its roundness was barely mentioned. It did not have to be. The quadrangles regarded the circle as "one of us."

The circle was well informed about the history of the quadrangles, about their attributes too. It knew, for example, that the sum of all the angles in a quadrangle equals 360 degrees, that all four sides were the same length, that all quadrangles had four right angles and four axes of symmetry, and that their diagonals were the same length, perpendicular to one another, and always halved. In fact, it was more of an expert on quadrangles than the quadrangles themselves. For the circle knew that they were really called "squares" and that there were actually other quadrangles that had different attributes. Why the other quadrangles in the community were not recognizable was rarely discussed. And neither was why the squares had occupied the name "quadrangle" for themselves alone. And that was probably why life was so good there.

One day another circle appeared in the community of quadrangles—a circle that did not disguise itself. Maybe it did not know that it should have done that. Or, and this is more likely, while it was meticulously well informed about the conditions of the community, it refused to apply the strategies of the first circle. Or continue to use them. In any case, it threatened to take forever for the two circles to find the courage and trust to meet—but eventually they managed it after all.

At some point, they encountered each other, each recognized itself in the other—along with their beautiful scars, along with their perfect quirks. For the first time in their lives, the two circles could just be themselves: complete and vulnerable.

They talked about a lot of things, and their shared vocabulary expanded to include wonderful new words such as "round" and "smooth." The word "corner" was not mentioned once. The circles rolled on the floor laughing until late into the night, until their edges trembled, until they could not cry anymore.

Consequently, the quadrangles wanted to get an easy-to-understand explanation the next day for why the circles had made so much noise during the night. The first circle tried to explain the matter with "round" and "smooth," but the quadrangles just looked aghast. The second circle twirled several times to depict the whole thing. But the quadrangles were still incapable of understanding, for the comfort of not-wanting-to-know is seductively and easily confused with a transient, superficial confusion. And since the circles would never again be like they had always been before, there was the threat of a split in the community. Many a square tear was shed.

Fortunately, there was a plan B. One of the quadrangles had traveled abroad once and discovered a completely new community of forms that called itself "triangles." Since the claim was that the circles were also somehow "different" and recognizably came from "somewhere else," they should be called "weird triangles." Even the circles themselves were happy with the new name. Too bad that they could not come up with a name for themselves on such short notice, but at least it was finally recognized that they had their own shape-identity.

Years later, in a community where many different shapes lived (of which most were still quadrangles), the "weird triangles" began to realize that the name "weird triangles" was actually completely wrong. They were not "weird triangles" but circles. And they were not "angle-less" or "non-angular" but "round" and "smooth." The debate over the new name was tedious. Many quadrangles made fun of the "weird triangles" and dismissed the whole thing as wordplay. They said that it did not matter what the words were as long as it was agreed that everyone meant the same thing with the words. Other quadrangles clamped onto the fact that the name "weird triangle" had come into being at a time when the word "weird" was not offensive and therefore could not be offensive now either. Some of the "weird triangles" were already too old or too aligned with the views of the quadrangles to care about these new-fangled circles. Why think about difference? All shapes were equal after all: all shape-lives mattered! Only a few of the quadrangles really took the circles seriously.

At some point in the distant future, circles, squares, triangles, quadrangles, rhombuses, and parallelograms will all live in a community in which everyone knows what "straight," "round," "curved," and "angular" mean. Each shape will have found a name for itself and will be able to communicate with one another without offending other shapes with its language.

Zafer Şenocak

Fore-Names

Translated by Lauren Beck

It was one of my grandfather's droll ideas to give me the name "Great Victory." Now, not only I but everyone who pronounces my name has waited for the past half century, that is as long as I have been in the world, for the great victory. It fails to materialize because we do not wage wars anymore. My grandfather, I cannot remember him since he died shortly after my birth, is said to have been a smart, well-traveled man. He probably suspected that in future lifetimes there would be no more victories and gave me this name not without some wistfulness. Or he was an incorrigible man who simply would not consider adapting to the times. No one gives that any thought today. No one can even imagine what a war means. In the history books, it always has something to do with expanding the size of our empire. An apple-sized country becomes first an orange, then a melon, after that formless, finally its borders reach all the way to the corners of the history book. Neighbors find no more room on the same page. That was our empire. And like every bloated thing, at some point it burst. We now live on one of its shreds and still fight amongst ourselves about what we should call this shred. I just call it "Shred." But a lot of people think this does not suit my name. "Great Victory" on a shred. One could also call this shred a shroud, for there is a particularly large number of corpses to be found here, subterraneously. At some point, cemeteries and gravestones were no longer laid out. At some point, one grew weary of the wars. This weariness was greater than the longing for victories.

So, according to my name, I am an outsider in this land. I remind the people of what they surrendered. Still, they are not unfriendly to me. For they certainly do not want to wage any wars. But then what do they do the entire day long? Do they not feel this itching all over their bodies? The burning under the soles of their feet? Is it not maybe time again to go to battle? At the very least, an encampment could be pitched, somewhere at the border. The point of borders, after all, is to let the good through and to stop the bad. We, however, let everyone through. We did not abolish only war but also the borders. Some probably thought that would be a cunning gambit to turn the shred into a great empire again. Yet the empire's border is no longer a border, either, after all. Someone is waging war against us. It is always war, we just hardly notice it, since we neither have an empire nor know borders, since we have come to terms with the fact that our borders are ignored and "Great Victory" is just a forename.

Someone calls for me and I come. I am an obedient soldier. Believe me, I only need a war to prove it. I need a war, a chance to prove myself.

III. Radio Play

Elfriede Jelinek

Ballad of Three Important Men and Also of the Circle of Persons Around Them, Dramatized for Radio

Translated by Elisabeth Fertig

Author's Introduction[1]

Transcribed and translated by Elisabeth Fertig

The roles are assigned, but we must play them ourselves. Or do the roles play us? Are we the ones being played in this card game? Do we get tossed onto the table, to lie there and wait in a sad pile until someone takes our trick, or perhaps we can take the trick ourselves? Do we have the trump card for once, or are we about to be had? In "Ballad of Three Important Men and Also of the Circle of Persons Around Them"—wherein the "Circle of Persons Around Them," as the title already indicates, represents a decorative accessory, the cloverleaf placed into the mouth of the slaughtered pig—the gender roles are assigned according to that good old cliché: The men are bold conquerors, brilliant artists, or brutish country boys. Their social circle consists of women, who are either sensual, homely, or otherwise not much. As clichéd as these roles seem, as much as we struggle against them, and as many voices constantly shout above the choir that everything has changed by now, that the roles have long been re-shuffled, that we are moving toward a new androgyny and so on, there is an entire industry working just as eagerly to immortalize and re-inscribe these roles, so that they can endlessly exploit them— that is, exploit us. Bodies do not serve to satisfy one another. No, bodies confronted with the beauty ideal of the advertising industry don't want to love one another but rather to shop. To shop for things that will enable them to play their role even better, to sell themselves even better. But they themselves are sold the more they try to increase their value through consumption. Regardless of whether it's a fancy woman buying fancy lingerie or a working housewife buying dish detergent off the supermarket shelf (the one that is allegedly also hand lotion), the goal is not satisfaction of desires but rather frustration, which gets converted back into the aggression of the purchase act. And just as desires are exploitable, so are bodies themselves, and

---

[1]Written and read by Elfriede Jelinek for a 1990 rebroadcast of *Ballad* as part of a retrospective of the author's Hörspiele ("hearing plays") on the German radio network SDR (Süddeutscher Rundfunk).

so is sexuality. "My sweater is so scratchy and raw just for you! I have a desire just for you!" says Jane to her Tarzan in the play. Sexual desire, inextricably coupled with gender roles—the man desires, the woman is desired—is reflected on store shelves. Desire materializes as its own stage props; desire itself becomes a prop. The prop is what counts. Without props, we won't be desired. Bodies must impose things on themselves, or they must hold a fast machine between their thighs, one that takes the form of a woman. (No car can be brought onto the market without the obligatory escort: a woman in lingerie, an evening gown, or a tight suit.) And finally, in an utter fetishization process, we become the decorative accessories ourselves, inanimate, irrelevant. The inanimate—the commodity—replaces the body, since the body, as has been suggested to us, can no longer exist without commodities. And, as the roles are pre-determined, so, too, are the clichés through which they express themselves, from textbooks to sappy TV love stories. What we call assertiveness in a man is called shrill hysteria in a woman. When a woman raises her voice to be heard, she needs to keep dialing it up. We then call it "nagging." I have investigated what happens when male and female actors swap lines and finally, in the end, when they swap roles—though it's clear that role and text are not the same, not identical with each other, not co-extensive. How does the same line of text sound when spoken by an actor or actress of the opposite gender? Maybe you'd like to hear for yourself.

Written in 1971; original broadcast March 17, 1974, co-produced by NDR/SDR, directed by Heinz Hostnig

> L   charles lindbergh
> W   anna, wife of charles lindbergh
> M1   male voice 1
> M2   male voice 2
> C   conductor
> B   ballet dancer
> T   tarzan
> J   jane
> K1   lindbergh's son (child's voice, younger)
> K2   tarzan's son (child's voice, somewhat older)

when the notation VOICE SWAP appears in the text, the characters should switch voices, so that the women's roles are spoken by men and vice versa. the notation VOICE SWAP always refers only to the two characters in whose dialogue it appears. the sound effects must contrast sharply with each other: e.g., the clattering of dishes for tarzan/jane, propeller noise for the lindberghs, and swan lake music for the conductor; but these can be modified at will. the tempo: quite brisk.

> L: mein name ist charles lindbergh, i have to get up soon. tomorrow will be a hard day, but it will also make me famous.[2]
> W: charles, please!
> L: i'm all packed up. tomorrow is the hard but beautiful day that will make me famous, therefore it will be hard, but not too hard.

---

[2]The decision to have Lindbergh introduce himself in German was made for two reasons: first, as a playful solution to the problem that this phrase is uttered in English in Jelinek's original and, second, to strengthen the glancing reference to Bertolt Brecht's 1929 Hörspiel *Ozeanflug*, which in its original version begins with the same phrase (that is, in German).

W: no, charles, please! don't do it! you can still change your
    mind. once you're in the air, you can't go back. think of
    our son!

L: i have to do it. there's an urge within me — to prove myself.
    i can't even tell you how strong the urge is at this very
    moment.

W: charles! no. think of the child! and if you won't think of the
    child, then please at least think of me.

L: this is something you can't understand. tomorrow i have to
    get up. you will never grasp the feeling of being the first to
    cross the great, wide ocean.

W: charles, god didn't create the ocean for you to die in and
    to leave me and the child alone. stay here, charles! there is
    still time.

L: you child! toward the end of this radio play, you will learn
    that nobody can hold back a person as deeply determined
    as i am.

W: charles! charles, stay here!

M1: no, take the darts in further here. and doesn't the color
    make me look pale?

M2: the color is just right. if it were even just the slightest bit on
    the bluer side, though, it might make you look pale.

M1: but even the green tones in it are making me look pale,
    right?

M2: if anything about this color is pale-making, it's not the
    green.

M1: actually, it would be good if the color made me a little
    paler, since i'm naturally blessed with rosy cheeks.

M2: exactly. and anyway, the red tones are taking things back in
    a less pale direction.

M1: do you find me pale?

M2: of course not. not too pale and not too rosy.

M1: my complexion is good, but it makes a slightly pale impres-
    sion, therefore: careful with the clothes!

M2: but this pattern in particular makes you look less pale than
    others i could name.

M1: well, in sunlight i always look less pale than in artificial light.

M2: but we're in the sun right now!

M1: exactly. and considering we're in the sun, i look much too pale. just imagine how pale i would look in artificial light.

M2: but you're not pale at all!

C: my name is famous conductor. i only conduct in the most famous opera houses and the greatest orchestras on earth. i also travel often and much. one must, in this trying career.

B: i'm only a small-time ballet dancer. i'm just starting out. there's a steep road ahead of me, a thorny one. my parents were a russian grand duke and duchess, they gave me the russian first name natasha. this increases my value somewhat.

C: when i am not conducting, i am resting from the acutely strenuous work of conducting. i am drained, spent to the last drop. sometimes i think about what the right word could be for what i am.

B: lonely is the word for what you are. i'm just starting out.

C: i am at home everywhere, i am always living out of my suitcase, which is strenuous and trying. fame costs me a lot, maybe too much. but when i'm standing before the berlin philharmonic, for example, i think to myself that fame in fact does not cost too much.

B: my career through the eyes of a woman: it is important, but not life itself, which is a completely different thing.

C: i have just now composed something to completion. i will continue composing right away: a ballet made of very modern music, which not many will understand, but that nevertheless will receive enthusiastic applause.

B: there's a tough road ahead of me. will i master it, or remain mediocre like so many others?

C: my music is so modern that not many can follow it. it can in no way be called mediocre.

B: i think i will remain mediocre like millions of others.

C: mediocrity is a big achievement for a woman but rather little for a man.

M1: light eye shadow makes my face look pale, more or less.

M2: no. anything but pale! for god's sake. then you should use dark ones.

M1: but even dark is sometimes pale-making.

M2: well, you're not pale, but it can't hurt to take precautions.

M1: but are you being honest when you say that you don't find me pale? today i am feeling truly pale.

W: charles! if you take off tomorrow, i'll leave you. i mean it.

L: but child! oh, you child. you know how much i love you, but you also know that a man has to prove himself wherever he goes and whatever he does.

W: charles, you have a child. don't forget that!

L: how could i forget something that makes up such a big part of my life, dear little wife, i will not forget you two. i will always have your image before my eyes as i cross the ocean. but i simply must cross, must ever be crossing.

W: (weeping) charles! do you know how a mother feels when her child will soon grow up without a father?

L: please don't cry. you ought to be brave and to believe in me. you ought to be proud of what i will achieve tomorrow. don't make this so hard for me, dear little wife.

W: charles, no!

K1: dad! dad! don't leave us, father, stay with us! don't you see how mom is crying?

L: my son. you can't understand it yet, but one day you will understand. then your father will be a hero. a famous flyer.

W: charles!

K1: father, stay with us.

L: my son, you're now the man of the house. take good care of your mother and return her to me just like i left her, in good condition!

K1: yes, father. i will look after mother. i promise.

W: charles! (sobs)

M1: then i'll look for a lipstick to match this dress, one that won't make me look pale.

M2: don't you think that this one will rather heighten than diminish the delicate tones of your face?

M1: i think that it will make me look pale.

M2: not at all! besides, you aren't pale in the least.

C: i have just finished conducting the composer stravin-sky's famous firebird suite. i am completely drained and depleted and sapped. but the applause is roaring.

B: i have just finished dancing my solo in the composer stra-vinsky's famous firebird suite. the great conductor was an artistic phenomenon. i felt as though he were supporting each of my steps, with this world-renowned music.

C: that little dancer has a so-called radiance that reached all the way to my conductor's podium, the loneliest place in the world.

B: i feel small next to him, insignificant, lost, and tiny. my parents left me a small apartment decorated with period furniture from the tsar's old palace. it would be the right setting for this extraordinary person and artist.

C: i am standing in front of the great entrance of the world-famous opera house. i am all alone. the music has left me all alone. i am standing in the rain, which is pattering down steadily and evenly, and gazing into the distance at my sports car, which i brought over from the united states.

B: my delicate dancer's body looks lost in this wide expanse. my hair is blonde and damp. i'm dead tired from the strain of the strenuous dance.

C: where are you going, you little, insignificant, lost, and tiny one?

B: to the left bank of the seine. that's where my small garçon-nière is, decorated with period furniture.

C: hello, sweet switchboard girl![3]

---

[3]German: "Hallo, du süße Klingelfee!" This is the first instance of a trope central to this text's intertextual strategy: all characters (men, women, and children) will spontaneously utter seemingly nonsensical one-liners that turn out to be the titles of kitschy, sentimental German and Austrian pop ballads (or *Schlager*) from the 1930s through the 1970s. I've made the decision to translate each title into English, more or less literally, while offering the original title in a footnote in the first instance of each. In the audio production of this *Hörspiel* that I worked with while creating this translation, these lines were always offset from the rest of the dialogue: for example, spoken more swiftly, more slowly, in a sing-song voice, or—in a notable use of stereophony—suddenly coming from the opposite channel

B: yes.

C: i've already picked up your small, delicate body so that your little shoes don't get wet. i've already taken this body in my conductor's arms and carried it over the puddles to my sports car, where i set it down with care.

B: how gentle a conductor's hands can be when they aren't tensely swinging a baton.

M1:   of the many things that can make one look pale, bright light is the worst.

M2:   but you aren't pale! of course, if the light is too bright . . .

M1:   do you find the light here too bright?

M2:   no, but i don't find you pale either.

M1:   are you trying to say that i'm imagining things?

M2:   of course not. in less bright light, i'm sure you're less pale.

T: my name is tarzan. between my jane and me, the athletically built man, there has been a noticeable amount of sexual tension.

J: the goats are milked, tarzan.

T: jane, take a rest! you manage your duties as a mother just as well as you manage your duties as a housewife.

J: i don't just want to be a good housewife and mother, i also want to be a good spouse. and yet, there is something unsatisfied within me — it festers.

T: what is this thing within you, jane, dear little train conductress?[4]

J: i'm afraid to tell you. the spouse within me says: be silent! but the housewife and mother within me say: speak!

T: say it, jane!

J: tarzan, don't you love me even one little bit?

T: i love the wife and mother within you, jane, but i also love the jane who is my wife and spouse.

K2:   on the farm. dad is driving the heavy combine. mom is in the kitchen, planning lunch with the farmgirl.

J: (sighs) i have a great big unsatisfied wish right now.

---

than the rest of the character's lines. Visit https://journals.publishing.umich.edu/absinthe/ to access a playlist of every song mentioned in this play.

[4]German: "Liebe kleine Schaffnerin."

T: tell me what it is. maybe i, the athletically built man, can help with my mixture of courage, strength, energy, vigilance, and experience.

J: tarzan, oh tarzan, that would be marvelous! you know how often i have to reach into the hot, greasy dishwater with my once-delicate hands, right?

T: tell me: how often, how often, jane? HOW OFTEN?

J: so i thought, tarzan, i thought it would be marvelous if we . . .

T: if we what? do tell me, jane!

J: if we (giggles)—i'm afraid to say it, my love. don't be so hard on your little wife!

T: jane, jane. you know that i, the athletically built man, believe it's better to be gentle than tough. come on, what is it?

J: you know that new lemon dish soap, honey, with the scent of ripe lemons?

T: the one that's supposed to make you wild and fresh? are you wild and fresh, jane?

J: no, i'm not, tarzan; that's just it. i haven't used it yet, but i have a desire for it. oh please, tarzan, please buy it! right now!

T: ok. i, the athletically built man, will buy it. and then there will be no more tension between us, jane? none?

J: no, tarzan, no! the mood is relaxed again now. in every marriage, there will be periods where tensions come up, but the clever and vigilant wife can always sway her lord and master with a bit of diplomacy.

K2: on the farm. father rides out with the farmhand. mother goes into the dairy to carry out housework.

W: you're not a mother, charles, you don't know what it means to lose the man you love. why are you always chasing adventure?

L: in any case, tomorrow is the difficult but big day that will bring me fame as the first ocean-crosser.

W: charles, you have so much to lose: both of us, myself and your child.

K1: don't cry, mother. i'm a man now. i'll protect you.

W: oh, my boy.

L: it must be so. i have to prove myself. tomorrow i will begin to prove myself. no one can stop me.

W: can you even look your child in the eyes anymore?

L: yes. i can look my child in the eyes precisely because tomorrow i am going to do my duty. you can't understand it. i have to get out there. i am a man. i must go onwards and upwards. soon i must go onwards and upwards. that is: tomorrow i must take off and prove myself, my little wife.

M1: hair, eye shadow, lipstick, nail polish, blush, makeup— everything, everything makes me pale!

M2: not at all! pale? no.

M1: perhaps this hat makes me less pale?

M2: much, much, much less.

M1: but still too pale, right?

M2: absolutely not, hardly a little bit pale.

M1: then only slightly pale, and yet still pale after all.

M2: hardly pale at all.

M1: then just a little bit pale, but still—pale.

B: no sooner am i carried to the car than i'm already in my apartment, surrounded by expensive textiles, furniture, and accessories. it's the right setting for this important person and artist who has come with me.

C: you seem almost a little lost here, while for me this is exactly the right setting. both for me as a person and for me as an artist. i'd like a drink now. i need something hard.

B: can i offer you a whiskey, neat—that means without water or ice, a real man's drink—out of this precious crystal bottle?

C: i'm drained from the strenuous work of conducting.

B: what a feeling it must be, to make the world submit to your will through music?

C: i call it the feeling of having passed a test. i am constantly composing, even when i am alone.

B: is it true that this work of conducting and composing must often be paid for with loneliness?

C: it is true, but one pays the price gladly. and yet the price is high. i kiss your hand, madame.[5]

B: exactly how high is the price that you must pay?

C: the high price that i must pay is called—my personal life. while others twiddle their thumbs, i compose modern compositions.

B: that is very high. but i think it's been worth it.

C: sometimes, when i'm standing dead tired in the limelight, with applause raining down on me, i think: a high price, but it's been worth it.

B: when i imagine never having children, never having a home . . . i would fall apart.

C: you supple willow: willows bend but don't break. but you're a woman after all—you and a home and children belong together. i kiss your hand, madame.

B: truly, i would fall apart. dear mediocrity!

C: perhaps you really would fall apart. i kiss your hand, madame.

B: within me, the woman is still battling the dancer within me.

C: within me, the artist within me has retained the upper hand, though not without a fight.

B: within me, the woman within me will retain the upper hand. no, wait! perhaps the dancer within me will gain the upper hand, after all!

C: if the dancer within you gained the upper hand, you'd no longer be a real woman. you would still be beautiful, but you would no longer be a woman—not a real, true one.

B: i think, i feel that i am still beautiful, though i am no longer a woman—not a real, true one.

VOICE SWAP

C: you are beautiful and have value as a person. and yet, your working life will soon leave its traces on your face, making

---

[5]German: "Ich küsse Ihre hand, Madame."

it tough and bitter. everything feminine and soft about it will disappear.

B: is there nothing left of the femininity and softness i once had?

C: the femininity as well as the softness is no longer what they once was. nevertheless, i myself am much harder and less valuable as a person, which is acceptable for a man and an artist. i, too, i think, feel torn.

B: let someone smooth out your worry lines. who can do that better than a woman?

C: your hands are no longer as soft as they once were. they've become tough and cracked by the struggles of life. hello, sweet switchboard girl!

B: you have luck with the ladies, bel ami.[6]

C: come to me! together we're less alone than one is when standing alone in the thundering applause under the limelight. i also happen to be looking for a title for my new, modern ballet. a new, modern title. i kiss your hand, madame!

L: mein name ist charles lindbergh. when i think of the ocean, then i instantly remember that i must prove myself tomorrow, as a man and as a flyer. tomorrow, i will take off with my brave little airplane.

W: charles, no! please! if you had ever been a mother, you wouldn't talk that way. a child needs his mother to dry his tears and his father to show him how to climb trees.

L: a man needs to know where he belongs.

W: you belong to your family, charles.

L: tomorrow i must take off, must prove myself. every man must.

K1: you don't understand it, mom! i'm the man now. i'll take good care of you, mom. i promised father i would.

L: anna, tomorrow i will take off. when the sun is up high, i'll be up high too.

W: charles, if you leave tomorrow, i'll leave you.

---

[6]German: "Du hast Glück bei den Frau'n, Bel Ami."

L: i have to! don't you understand that? when a man says he must, he must.

T: jane, there's a cheeky curl peeking out of your scarf. only a woman's curl could peek out of her scarf like that. dear little train conductress.

J: oh tarzan! it's hardly cheeky.

T: and how your body is outlined under that thin sheath! only a woman's body could be outlined under a thin sheath like that.

J: oh tarzan, hardly! it's not outlined at all. my sweater is scratchy and raw.

T: i, the athletically built man, see no scratchy sweater, i only see your fit body underneath it. with brand new eyes.

J: oh, tarzan, my sweater is so scratchy and raw just for you!

T: be quiet! let me, the athletically built man, gaze at you quietly!

J: my love, i have a brand new desire. i have this beautiful brand new desire just for you. but my sweater is still scratching me, ow, it's scratchy just like the towels.

T: what kind of desire is that, jane? haven't you always gotten everything you wanted? what kinds of new desires are these? dear little train conductress.

J: i think it's more of a physical desire. do you think we could today, tarzan? please! i'll cook your favorite food. you have luck with the ladies, bel ami.

T: no, jane, no! you're a woman, you should only want to give, never take. you know: giving is more blessed than taking. do you want to get old and used up before your time? to no longer be attractive to me, the athletically built man? to lose your femininity?

VOICE SWAP

J: tarzan, i think my femininity just went missing. i have a desire, tarzan. you have luck with the ladies, bel ami.

K2: on the farm. father is balancing the books. mother is sitting in a corner and mending stockings, socks, and various other things that her wild boys have ripped up. monika, her youngest, is helping diligently. outside, her older brothers hans and erwin are running and climbing around. they're racing to the top of the highest cherry tree.

J: tarzan, my sweater is so raw just for you, ow. it leaves me with an unsatisfied feeling—a similar feeling to the one you leave me with, tarzan. lonely boy . . . [7]

T: the one thing that i, the athletically built man, loved most about you, jane, was your femininity. jane, you're not as feminine as you once were, and far, far less feminine than you could be if you tried. think about it! did you do everything you could to make your sweater both white and soft? dear little train conductress.

J: no! what a harsh, dissonant screech. for god's sake, no!

T: just add a capful of fabric softener to the last wash cycle.[8] poor little ingeborg.[9]

K2: on the farm. father is still balancing the books. mother is still sitting in the corner, but now she's praying the rosary. moni, her youngest, is doing her best to follow along. outside, the wild brothers hans and erwin are running around.

C: you are beautiful. you radiate a certain something that only a woman can radiate.

---

[7] German: "Einsamer Boy."

[8] This line comes from a series of 1970s TV commercials for Lenor fabric softener. In one, a beautiful housewife is admonished by her "conscience" (who appears in the ad as her double) for not getting the laundry soft or white enough. But when she adds a capful of Lenor to the last cycle, as her conscience instructs her, everything is set right. The last line in the ad is the woman's conscience telling her, as she happily arranges flowers, "Everyone loves you so much." Austrian listeners in the 1970s (especially women) would likely have caught this right away, as my mother did when she listened to the radio production of this text.

[9] Like the other intertextual scraps, this line jumps out because it appears to have no context at all. Who is Ingeborg? Austrian readers and listeners would likely think of Ingeborg Bachmann, perhaps the best-known woman author in Austrian literary history. The link is strengthened by details of Bachmann's biography and reception, notably the public fascination with her relationships with famous male artists, including Paul Celan and Max Frisch. For all her achievements, Bachmann still tends to be read through her love life. Jelinek is also a prominent interpreter of Bachmann's work and wrote the screenplay for the 1991 film of Bachmann's only complete novel, *Malina*.

B: ha, i'm hardly beautiful.

C: i would liken you to an old renaissance painting, if i weren't so busy with my bold, modern composition. what title can i give it? i can't think of a single one that would be new and bold enough.

B: let me think about it, please! maybe i can . . .

C: no, don't think about it. you've already lost enough of that femininity that i used to love so much about you. where has it gone? as for me, i'm pure male toughness, while you're still more feminine and softer than i am, despite greater toughness than you used to have.

B: i think "abandoned" would be a pretty title.

C: ha! that title is much too feminine. i kiss your hand, madame. i'm thinking "passion" would be a good title, or even "passion in the pond."

B: i will grow as an artist, although it will count against me as a woman. as for that title: it's cheap. what about "swan lake"?

C: you have a lot of work to do on yourself, whereas i'm already complete. but the title is good. may it always remind me of you, my little one. a tough, masculine line has just etched itself into the corner of your mouth, which counts against your femininity.

B: yes, i feel it now, this tough, masculine line.

C: i will compose my famous ballet, swan lake, and you will dance the female lead. this will be part of my sponsorship of your talents. any moment, the melodies will start flowing out of me.

(music: swan lake)

B: could it be true, really true, that the melodies are already flowing? isn't swan lake too great for you? won't you fail?

C: a woman must believe in her man, or he'll lose his grip. regardless, my modern music will be even more modern than the title swan lake could ever suggest.

B: OUR swan lake.

C: my swan lake. this work will become even bolder and more modern through your interpretative talents.

B: sometimes i think it will never be written, this ballet. will it come between us?

C: often career stress is what comes between a man and a woman. everyday life does the rest. i kiss your hand, madame.

B: even i often doubt myself. the tough, masculine line at the corner of my mouth is proof.

C: well, i do not doubt myself at all.

B: you're a man. swan lake is calling you. never look back, always ahead.

C: i kiss your hand, madame. there's an urge within me to compose this modern ballet, i can't help it. it urges and urges.

B: you have luck with the ladies, bel ami!

W: i'll fight for you, charles. weak as i am, i removed a screw from the motor of your plane. you can't take off tomorrow. i hereby rebel for the last time.

L: give it here, you little dumb-dumb, that's not for you to mess with. hello, sweet switchboard girl!

VOICE SWAP

W: my will is rebelling, which you can see because my face is twisted into a white mask of determination. i threw the screw in the trash, charles, out of hatred for that plane.

L: (stuttering) it will take a day, uh, one whole day, anna, for me to find a replacement. the takeoff can't be saved. masculine toughness and determination are written across your face. where is the softness that i always loved so much about you? dear little train conductress?

W: at the moment, i'm nothing but toughness. i want you to stay, charles, with me and with our son.

K1: mother, i'm a man now, i'll take care of you.

L: actually, a harmonious family life is the greatest joy in the world. i've come late to this realization, but not too late, anna. i'll stay with you two, my love. many adventurers, cowboys, explorers, artists, and scholars have realized this before me.

W: charles, you're making too little of yourself. you could achieve far more, charles, if you would just make a serious effort!

L: i did like to kiss the ladies. dear little train conductress!

W: i love my family, too, charles, maybe even more than you do. but there's no way a man can seek and find his greatest joy at home with his family. whereas i, as a wife and a mother, can certainly find my greatest joy, my inner happiness as a wife and a mother, with my family. you must take off tomorrow, charles! your brave airplane can be a wife and child to you. lonely boy . . .

L: i think the word for what you are is ruthless. i did like to kiss the ladies. is my son supposed to grow up without a father? he'll be grown soon. is he supposed to come of age without me? you're a mother. you've borne a child. can't you understand me? dear little train conductress.

W: tomorrow is your big day, my love! aren't you looking forward to it? tomorrow, your battle with the elements begins, which will make you into a famous man. charles, the screw . . . it was never removed. i just wanted to test you, charles. you have luck with the ladies, bel ami!

L: what? (stuttering) anna, yes it was. the screw—it was removed! it was! i watched you do it myself!

W: no, charles, my love, i didn't remove it. i lied. i lied for you. forgive me.

K1: i'm a man now, mother. don't be afraid, i'll protect you!

L: let me stay with you, anna! my love!

W: you must! that word might as well have been made for men. tomorrow, you must take off.

L: but my child is calling out to me. i think i must hear that call.

K1: father, let mother go. take off with integrity!

L: no, let me stay with you! adventure no longer calls to me when i look into your clear eyes.

B: and so another night fades, and i'm fading too.

C: it was a lovely night.

B: and now off to your desk, to swan lake!

C: it was a lovely night. if it was lovely for you, then it was lovely for me too. do you think my ballet, swan lake, is already calling to me?

B: it is calling loudly, my love. on my many tours i've experienced considerably lovelier nights than this, yet you could still call it a pretty nice one.

C: if only my desk weren't calling! i want to stay with you always.

B: for example, under the southern cross i once experienced a night that was considerably lovelier than this one.

C: i want to stay with you always and never go back to my cold, hard desk.

B: did you know that i'm married?

C: no, no! not married!

B: my husband lives in the states, in a sanatorium, incurable.

C: no, not incurable! at the moment i think it's too much for me, though presently i will notice that it's not too much. i must abstain—as a man, a conductor, and a composer.

B: abstinence is good for your artistic maturity. you are writing this modern ballet for me, and while you write, you will abstain from me (singing: aaaah) our swan lake! (music)

C: i am already abstaining. it has become second nature to me.

B: you have luck with the ladies, bel ami! this swan lake is sounding familiar to me.

C: you're getting that impression because it will become a famous ballet. my beloved little ballerina. i kiss your hand, madame.

B: i've just sewn a loose button back onto your tuxedo jacket. the button came loose from the strenuous work of conducting. sometimes the woman within me demands her rights, despite being hidden away.

C: i kiss your hand, madame. despite your substantial toughness, sometimes the woman in you blooms like a flower in the wilderness.

B: compose, compose away! we can never see each other again.

C: inwardly i've already abstained, but the task is now proving difficult, almost as difficult as swan lake. thank you for fixing that small and inconspicuous seam!

B: you're very welcome. sometimes i think swan lake is neither bold nor modern.

C: oh yes it is, my love. please, say swan lake is bold and modern! please! don't crush my last shred of enthusiasm for my work!

M1: the darkness always makes me so pale, don't you think?

M2: yes, i think so too. i can hardly see you.

M1: that's a lie! i'm not the least bit pale today. you'd be glad to have my face.

J: oh, tarzan, how clumsy! coffee stains on the nice white tablecloth.

T: jane, i'm sorry. just now i, the athletically built man, have soiled the nice white tablecloth. now there's a nasty little dirt goblin all over the lily-white tablecloth. us men are sometimes big and clumsy like that—but that's why you love us, right, janie?

J: tarzan, i don't love you at all and your clumsiness is getting on my nerves. what are we going to do now?

T: jane, you don't love me anymore! (sobs) you don't love me, the herculean man, anymore! here is the laundry detergent, jane. will you love me again if i wash the tablecloth?

J: no, and i still wouldn't love you even if you had brought me the pre-wash detergent instead of this hot wash detergent. because i'm about to say this: it's clean, but it wasn't properly pre-soaked.

T: jane! will you still not love me ever again (sobs) even if i, the athletically built man, use the pre-wash detergent? even then?

K2: on the farm. father is negotiating with the hog trader. mother has a big laundry day today. the farmgirl is helping her. how those little rascals get everything dirty! smiling, mother shakes her head kindly. then she gets back to work.

T: truly lily-white! look, jane! consoled, i sniffle through my nose. now you surely love me, the herculean man, again, jane. (crash, shards) oh, jane, what have you done! (sobs) coffee stains on the lily-white tablecloth again! now i, the athletically built man, have to go do the laundry again. but i do it gladly and with pleasure. for you, jane.

J: well, at least it WAS lily-white, tarzan. haha.

K2: on the farm. father is driving the wagon into town. he has some business to take care of. mother is sitting in god's corner and sewing herself a new blouse. wait, no! the blouse isn't for her, it's for her little daughter, monika. mother never works for herself: when she moves her diligent hands, it's always for others. monika is sitting next to mother on a stool and sewing a doll's dress. our kind mother helps her often, because moni is still little. soon, susi the doll will have a pretty, new, red dress. hopefully those wild boys won't ruin it again.

C: now the melodies are flowing through me again. with such intensity and abundance—like never before. i kiss your hand, madame.

B: it must be an unusual feeling, to have melodies flowing through you. this swan lake is seeming more and more familiar to me.

C: impossible. it's bold, modern, and yet universally accessible. i'll conduct it myself too. i kiss your hand, madame.

B: when i dance, something flows from my body. something indefinable, a mixture of spirit and body.

C: a great deal flows from your body: artistic talent.

B: even you are talented somehow, much as i doubt it whenever i hear swan lake. but it's no reason to despair!

C: no, no reason. i'm summoning new courage as we speak. how do you like this? (sings swan lake theme)

B: it's just not new, not unique. i'm beginning to understand your doubts about your talents more and more.

C: i did like to kiss the ladies. only the legs of dolores do that.[10]

B: we have a shared goal: our world-renowned ballet.

C: i'll flee from you like a deer from a hunter.

---

[10]German: "Das machen nur die Beine von Dolores."

B: i'll pursue you and overtake you. i am a woman, you are a man. could there be a more fortuitous coming-together?

C: i have to abstain from you. for the first time since i lost my dear parents, i'm abstaining from something. swan lake, i'm coming! a song goes 'round the world.[11]

B: this song thing—if i were you, i'd think long and hard about it.

C: do you mean that i could be no more than a minor, interpretative talent? no, you can't mean that! not in light of swan lake, the bold and modern work.

B: sure, you're a little talented. but too little for swan lake.

C: may i just sit still here for a little while longer and gaze at you?

B: yes, but you must be very still. no humming, singing, or whistling swan lake!

L: anna! we'll see if you don't regret this one day. our child may also regret it. don't you think?

W: you don't understand, charles. take off! this is your duty.

L: but just look into our child's eyes. how he begs and pleads. it's my child too, anna!

W: when i look into the eyes of our son and heir i waver for the blink of an eye, but i hold fast. tomorrow, you must take off!

L: don't deprive our child of a father, anna!

W: would you be proud of a man who broke a promise he had made to himself, charles?

L: a woman can only be proud of a man who wouldn't break a promise he had made to himself.

W: good boy, keep thinking that way. and now: onwards and upwards!

L: there's more to life than pride, anna.

W: you have luck with the ladies, bel ami. lonely boy . . . tomorrow you'll push through the clouds with your flying body.

K1:   father, come on, don't cry. i'll protect mother!

---

[11]German: "Ein Lied geht um die Welt."

J: tarzan, you said we could do it after dinner.

T: i don't feel like it, jane! (giggling) we men have our lit-
      tle weaknesses. and for me, the athletically built man, it's
      alcohol.

J: tarzan, i'm a woman. i have desires.

T: do you still love me, jane?

J: i'm about to just reach out and grab you! you have luck
      with the ladies, bel ami.

T: first tell me if you still love me even a little, jane!

J: unfortunately, i don't love you at all, tarzan. (tarzan sobs)
      oh, christ!

T: my jane doesn't love me, the athletically built man, any-
      more. (weeps)

K2:   on the farm. father is scolding the farmhand. mother is
      smiling as she watches her wild boys climb the cherry tree.
      monika sits on the ground below, talking to her doll.

J: it's up to us women to awaken the good in a man or make
      him into a murderous beast.

W: tomorrow you'll take off, charles, so that you can keep
      being yourself, and so i can be proud of you. you will only
      be yourself if you take off tomorrow, charles.

L: i'm so afraid! hello, sweet switchboard girl.

W: you would be unfaithful to yourself if you stayed tomorrow.

L: maybe not so unfaithful, anna. please say that i wouldn't
      be unfaithful to myself if i stayed on the ground tomorrow,
      anna!

W: i can't lie like that, charles.

L: anna, i have to confess something to you: i removed a
      screw from the motor of my plane. i can't even take off
      tomorrow. i hereby rebel for the last time.

W: give it here, you little dumb-dumb!

L: i threw the screw in the trash, anna. i'll never find it again.
      hello, sweet switchboard girl!

W: it will take a day to find a replacement, charles.

L: anna! just let me stay with you. pretty please.

W: you could have endangered yourself and your plane with
      your recklessness, charles.

L: i'm so ashamed, anna, so very ashamed. can you forgive me?

W: well, the day after tomorrow you really must take off. stupid, senseless charles!

K1:   mother, i'm a man now. i'll take care of you.

L: please, let me stay here, anna! you're my wife! please!

B: swan lake didn't amount to anything this time around either. nothing bold, nothing modern.

C: i'm going to go now, to make swan lake even greater and more modern than it already is.

B: you're better off practicing your conducting!

C: the critics will not understand my revolutionary ideas— but you, you will understand me. the only one in europe or abroad who will understand. i kiss your hand, madame.

B: well, at this point i still don't understand it at all. but work hard, as hard as you can.

C: i will mature in my art. mature for you. i kiss your hand, madame.

B: will swan lake mature too?

C: it, too, will mature over the years. i can become much more mature as a person too, if i try. then swan lake will automatically mature along with me. i kiss your hand, madame, and mistake it for your mouth. you're so charming, madame! (pause)

L: anna, about the screw . . .

W: yes, charles?

L: it's not true, anna, i lied again, anna, forgive me, please. i didn't want to lose you, so i tried a miserable trick. dear little train conductress. i did like to kiss the ladies.

W: ok, so tomorrow, then. tomorrow you really must take off, charles.

L: forgive me, anna, if you still can. i'm so ashamed. i did like to kiss the ladies. dear little train conductress.

W: yes, charles, you're right. shame on you! be ashamed! it's good for you.

L: forgive me, anna!

K1:   mother, i'm the man now, i will take care of you. dear little train conductress. hello, sweet switchboard girl, i did like to kiss the ladies, only the legs of dolores do that . . . etc., etc.

VOICE SWAP again (from this point, all characters swap voices once more—so that the male roles are again voiced by men and female roles by women—until the end)

T: oh, jane, you aren't having secret desires again, are you? with my arts and crafts corner calling to me and my jigsaw collecting dust?

J: yes, tarzan, i have a great, unsatisfied desire. come with me!

T: oh, jane, dear little train conductress, you yourself gave these lovely art supplies to me, the herculean man! so that i could craft all kinds of pretty things, like this proverb i wrote with a wood-burning pen.

J: you're coming with me, tarzan! you're going to satisfy my sexual demands this instant!

T: oh, jane. i, the athletically built man, have such a headache! only the physical exertion of using my new hammer drill helps. please, jane, dear little train conductress!

J: tarzan!! you will come right now!

T: no, jane, please! let me solve this difficult crafting problem. please, please, jane. i enjoy it so much. i'm sure that this original craftwork will please you, too, when it's finished. but there's still a lot of work left to be done. i did like to kiss the ladies.

J: tarzan!!! will you come here! (fade out)

C: (humming swan lake) and this theme still needs to be cleaned up, and this little spot. this wrinkle in the cantilena still needs to be ironed out. only the legs of dolores do that.

B: i get the sense i've heard this dumb swan lake not just once but many times before.

C: no way! too bold, too modern. i made it that way. i did like to kiss the ladies.

B: did you know that swan lake possibly already exists, you idiot?

C: impossible! too bold. too modern. before me: no swan lake. with me: swan lake. after me: nothing but swan lake. i kiss your hand, madame.

B: to hell with your swan lake!

C: swan lake no hell but hope for many. this is goal of art. also my goal. (sings swan lake)

B: dear god, what nonsense!

W: what are you holding so tightly behind your back, charles?

L: i can't tell you, dear little train conductress.

W: what is it, charles?

L: it's nothing (stuttering) nothing . . . nothing, anna!

W: give it here right now! this is . . . this is . . .

L: a little screw, anna, dear little train conductress.

W: this just can't be true, charles.

L: it is true. i removed it from my airplane myself.

W: will you put it right back where you found it, charles?

L: no (sniffs), please no, anna! please! think of our child, anna!

W: do you want to make me angry, charles?

L: no, anna, please don't be angry with charles! (weeps) i didn't mean it that way, anna. watch, i'm screwing it back into its rightful place. are you still angry, anna?

W: i'm still very annoyed, charles. what will you do early tomorrow morning?

L: (crying) i'll take off, anna.

W: what was that, charles?

L: (crying) tomorrow i must take off. (sobbing uncontrollably) i did like to kiss the ladies, dear little . . . don't be angry, please, please, anna! i'll never do it again. i promise.

W: i'm still very annoyed, charles. but you can make up for your mistake today by being extra diligent tomorrow.

L: (sobbing uncontrollably) dear little train conductress, hello, sweet switchboard girl . . . (fade out)! (long pause)

M1 & M2: have you finally noticed any changes to your physical person? if yes, then these have always been present in you. they are of completely natural origin and will influence your organism only insofar as they are decisive for the victory or defeat of your character. they are thus no cause for concern. have you finally . . . (repeat and gradually fade out)

Elisabeth Fertig

Translator's Reflection

Ballad of Three Important Men is a "Hörspiel" by the Nobel-Prize-winning Austrian poet, essayist, novelist, and playwright Elfriede Jelinek, originally titled *Für den Funk dramatisierte Ballade von drei wichtigen Männern sowie dem Personenkreis um sie herum,* and written for broadcast on German radio in 1974. "Hörspiel" (plural "Hörspiele") is a word I intentionally leave untranslated. In more or less literal terms, it means something like "hearing play," but that doesn't quite capture the full meaning. Though its closest equivalent in Anglophone literature is the radio play, the Germanophone Hörspiel is historically and aesthetically distinct from its nearest counterparts in other language traditions. To this day, many well-known German and Austrian writers have had Hörspiele produced on the radio, often written in the early stages of their careers and thus influencing their later work. The Hörspiel is regarded as a major literary genre and encompasses a rich tradition of audio-poetic innovation and experimentation, whose media-specific themes and methods can be seen to have flowed back into German literary aesthetics in general.

Chief among the many challenges of this project was the deceptively simple question: What exactly is the source text of a Hörspiel translation? In other words, when translating a literary genre whose primary form is the acoustic event of a radio broadcast, where do we locate the work? To admit that the answer to this question is not immediately obvious, more than just presenting a technical obstacle, can also open space for literary- and media-theoretical contemplation, as well as illuminate provocative questions about the nature of translation. Typically, a Hörspiel begins as a script—words on a page—which may be either published in book form or may be available to researchers only as a manuscript in an archive, if at all. In this case, I've relied on a script of *Ballade* published in 1980 by the press of a small art gallery near Munich called Kunstraum Schwifting. Along with this text, I've worked with an archival mp3 recording of the 1974 premiere production on West German radio, running just over 45 minutes long. This audio production diverges from the script in interesting ways. For example, the production rearranges the script substantially—even changing the order of certain scenes. Why was this done? Was it to accentuate the impact or increase the legibility of the "voice swap" scenes, where the male and female voice actors suddenly switch roles? In the use of music and sound effects, while following the stage directions in the script, the production also makes notable interpretive choices; for example, the recurring musical motif of the theme from Swan Lake is sometimes distorted, looped, or abruptly started and stopped at full volume without fading, rendering it uncanny and sinister and underscoring the sense of entropy that animates the piece.

Finally, in the cryptic last monologue, spoken by the characters identified as male voice 1 and male voice 2, the stage directions indicate only that the voices should "repeat and gradually fade out," but in the recording there is much more going on. The first time they speak the line, the voices take turns. Then they begin to chant in unison, and each time they repeat the line, their voices get just a little louder, a little faster, and a little angrier. By the end, we hear them practically screaming the words, just as the prescribed fade-out begins to mute their impotent rage. Provisionally, prioritizing readability, I've left such production choices largely undocumented in my translation, with a few exceptions. But one can equally imagine an alternative or future version of this project that uses the recording, and not the script, as its primary source text. How might the translator choose to represent in written form what in the source work is not read, but heard? Perhaps the proper form for this translation would not be a printed text at all, but a radio production.

In asking questions like these, we might notice that a production of a Hörspiel is *already* a sort of translation: the director, producer, composer, voice actors, engineers, editors, etc., are the translators who take the author's written source text and convert it from a work of written language into an acoustic text, from the medium of print into radio. In this respect, the Hörspiel bears much in common with adjacent forms like stage drama, and especially with film and television, though it is distinct in that its action unfolds purely in the acoustic realm, and its associated conventions for criticism and academic study are less well established. As with any work of translation, there is no single or straightforward way to go about it: even a script with the most abundant and detailed stage directions must be interpreted. The dream of a "faithful" interpretation of the script, as with any translation, ultimately reveals itself as a utopian or even authoritarian fantasy: even where the production follows the script as closely as possible, it is constructed from a series of choices and takes on a life over and above the text on which it is based. In fact, Jelinek is famous for leaving production details up to the director's interpretation, especially in her stage dramas, as indicated by her iconic stage direction: "machen Sie was Sie wollen" ["do what you want"]. This move not only emphasizes the inherently translational nature of performing a written script but helps destabilize the traditional categories of author and work entirely, opening out onto a fundamentally dynamic and collaborative conception of the text.

There is another major aspect of this piece that comes across more fully in the audio production than in the written script: it's funny. Harsh critics of Jelinek's often shockingly grotesque poetics tend to miss the comic or satiric register, maybe owing in part to the inevitable translation problems and lack of familiarity with the historical Austrian context with which she's in conversation. But in working on this project and in the frame of my larger dissertation research on the Hörspiel, I have come to believe that Jelinek's humor, like her language in general, reaches its most profound unfolding when performed. I read the script first, but it was only while listening to the audio that I laughed out loud.

The most obvious source of humor in this Hörspiel is the confusion caused by the increasingly denaturalized gender relationships initially set in motion by the "voice swap." However, it's my sense that the awkward, stilted dialogue is the bedrock on which the rest of the comedy builds. The characters parrot stock phrases, repeat themselves ad absurdum, blurt out song titles and generally sound unnatural. In this translation, I've sought to at least preserve and at times even amplify this effect. For instance, I chose to translate the out-of-place song titles more or less literally into English, rendering them all the more strange. I hope that readers (especially first-time readers of Jelinek) will have patience with the range of negative affects—from confusion to irritation to fatigue to revulsion—that wading through such alienated language might elicit. I believe there is value in staying with the discomfort of a disorienting aesthetic encounter like this one. A funny thing can happen when reading any text in translation, as when speaking a foreign language: the illusion of smoothness and sense more readily falls away, exposing the ideological trusswork holding idiomatic language together. The weirdness that ensues can be a punchline and epiphany at once. If you get stuck, I recommend reading it aloud.

Contributors

Abdullah Alqaseer was born in Salamiyah, Syria, and has published a number of essays as well as a short story collection, *Nackt im AlAbbasseen*, and a novel, *Gebrauchte Alpträume*. He now lives in Halle, Germany, and continues to write. "A Lie Named Germany" was translated by Mustafa Al-Slaiman for *Weiter Schreiben (Writing On)*, a project that seeks to provide a platform for authors originally from countries that are currently plagued by war or other crises, enabling them to continue writing, publishing, and finding readers for their work. Thus, *Weiter Schreiben* typically presents texts in multiple languages—in this case Arabic and German—enabling different points of linguistic entry.

Lauren Beck is a PhD candidate in the Department of Germanic Languages and Literatures at the University of Michigan. Her dissertation project examines temporal aesthetics and experiences in contemporary (post-)socialist fiction, focusing particularly on memory exchange between generations of women. Her past research has addressed visual culture and photography, modernism, German-language Soviet wartime propaganda, North American Finns in Soviet Karelia, Russian migration to Berlin in the 1920s, and other topics.

Elisabeth Fertig is a writer, translator, and PhD candidate in Comparative Literature at the University of Michigan, where her research focuses on the intersection of experimental poetics and radio drama in English and German. Additional research areas include sound studies, media theory, audio storytelling, feminist and queer theory, contemporary poetics, critical translation studies, and autotheory. She earned her BA in English and German from Oberlin College and currently hosts a weekly radio show on WCBN-FM, Ann Arbor's freeform community radio station. Previously, Elisabeth served two years on *Absinthe*'s managing editorial team.

Ivan Parra Garcia is a fiction writer, translator, and third-year PhD student in Comparative Literature at the University of Michigan. His academic interests relate to the intersections of theory and experience and philosophy and literature. He received an MFA in Spanish Creative Writing at the University of Iowa. His collection of short stories, titled *Texarkana*, was published by Sudaquia Editores (New York) in 2021.

Catalin Dorian Florescu was born in Timişoara, Romania, and has been living in Switzerland since 1982. "In the Navel of the World," initially published in 2001, follows an unnamed narrator's reminiscences about his journey from Romania to Switzerland— one that is notably similar to Florescu's own experience. Considering questions of nostalgia, belonging, translation, and more, "In the Navel of the World" is just the very beginning of Florescu's wider oeuvre. Since its publication, Florescu has authored six novels, a collection of short stories, and numerous essays. Among them are *Der Mann, der das Glück bringt* (The man who brings happiness, 2016) and "Ich muss Deutschland" (I must Germany, 2017), the latter of which was adapted for the stage in 2020. He has received literary prizes such as the Adelbert von Chamisso Prize (2002), the Swiss Literature Prize (2011), and the Andreas Gryphius Literature Prize (2018), as well as many others.

Marina Frenk was born 1986 in Chişinău, Moldova, and immigrated to Germany in 1993. She studied acting at the Folkwang Academy in Essen and played from 2008 to 2015 in permanent engagements at subsequently held engagements in the company of the Bochum Theatre, the Centraltheater Leipzig, the Cologne Theatre, and Maxim Gorki Theater Berlin, among others. She made her cinema debut in *Totem* by Jessica Krummacher. She was the lead singer of the folk-gypsy band Kapelsky and the electro-dance band The Real Baba Dunyah. Her debut novel, *ewig her und gar nicht wahr* (long ago but not really true), was published in 2020.

Lena Grimm is a third-year PhD student at the University of Michigan's Department of Comparative Literature. Her work currently focuses on the reception and translation of ancient Greek tragedy in contemporary German and English language contexts. Having initially encountered the Swiss variety of the language through her family, she has long been interested in the plurality of Germans that exist within the Germanophone world.

Barbara Honigmann was born in East Berlin in 1949. She established herself as an influential German-Jewish writer thanks to her plays, essays, and novels that explore her relationship with Jewish and German culture and history in the twentieth century. Honigmann's parents left Germany for England during the Second World War and returned to East Berlin at the end of the war. Honigmann studied theater at Humboldt University. After living for many years under a socialist regimen, she immigrated to Strasbourg, France, where she developed her career as a prose writer and established her new residence. Honigmann continued to engage with Jewish-German history and the cultural changes experienced among the new generations. Her work problematizes traditional ideas of identity and resists conventional ideas of national literature and art. Honigmann has received literary prizes for her works, such as the Kleist Prize in 2000 and the Koret Jewish Book Award in 2004. The essays included in this issue are part of her 1998 book, *Am Sonntag spielt der Rabbi Fußball* (On Sunday the rabbi plays soccer). In this collection of "sketches," Honigmann presents us with her experience of meeting a highly diverse Jewish community in Strasbourg. This book explores the beauty and power of everyday life from a writer's perspective that creates her art from her encounter with tradition and change, the transnational and the local, the personal and the communal.

Elfriede Jelinek is an Austrian author best known for her novels and plays but whose extensive body of work also includes poetry, essays, and radio drama. Born in Styria, Austria, in 1946, she studied music from an early age and graduated from the Vienna Conservatory before beginning her literary career. She has said that her musical training has had a strong impact on her writing. In 2004, she was awarded the Nobel Prize in Literature, "for her musical flow of voices and counter-voices in novels and plays that with extraordinary linguistic zeal reveal the absurdity of society's clichés and their subjugating power." Befitting the public controversy with which Jelinek is often associated, one member of the Swedish Academy resigned in protest of the decision. Jelinek is known for her radical leftist political views regarding the interplay of language, power, gender, capital, sex, and violence in Austria—expressed in her literary work as well as in speeches, interviews, and essays. She is also active as a translator and co-authored the 1981 German translation of Thomas Pynchon's novel *Gravity's Rainbow*. Though Jelinek is one of the most famous and highly decorated living authors of German literature, she is less known in the English-speaking world, in part due to the relative scarcity of published English translations of her work to date.

Özlem Karuç is a translator, teacher, and PhD candidate in the Department of Germanic Languages and Literatures at the University of Michigan. Her research focuses on literature and film dealing with the German Exile Era (1933–1945) and with questions of migration, exile, race, and ethnicity in postwar Germany. Currently, she is examining the intersectionalities of Black German and Turkish German identities as (self-)represented in literature and film, against the backdrop of how Germanness has been configured from the fall of the Wall to the present. Özlem recently translated over fifty art songs and all related concert programs for Elbphilharmonie Hamburg's concert series Song of America: A Celebration of Black Music. Her translations were used in program printouts and as subtitles for the recordings of the concerts available as online streams.

Michaela Kotziers is a PhD student in English and Women's and Gender Studies at the University of Michigan. Her research focuses on phenomenological experiences of gender and sexuality, women's life writing, and lesbian feminist politics.

Ronnith Neumann is a Jewish-German writer and photographer whose work explores geographical and linguistic displacement, postwar German Jewish identity, and the relationship of tradition and change in late twentieth-century Germany. Neumann was born in Israel in 1948. At the age of ten, she immigrated with her family to Germany. She would train as a photographer, work in the Norddeutscher Rundfunk in Hamburg, and develop her manifold writing career. She explores "the possibilities for renegotiating the parameters of a specifically German-Jewish identity in post-Shoah Germany" and raises questions of home, origins, ruptures, and displacements. Her literary work of more than four decades includes plays, novels, and short stories. She has received numerous awards, including the Hamburg

Literature Prize for Short Prose in 1986, the Gladbecker Satirepreis in 1989, and the Herford Culture Prize in 1995.

Ronya Othmann is a poet, novelist, and journalist living in Leipzig, Germany. She grew up in Landkreis Freising with her Yazidi-Kurdish father and German mother. In 2014, she began her studies at the German Literature Institute in Leipzig. Her poetry has appeared in several anthologies and journals, and her debut novel, *Die Sommer* (The summer), was published in 2020 by Hanser Verlag and shortlisted for the Aspekte-Literaturpreis. Othmann won the Ingeborg Bachmann Prize Audience Award in 2019 for her essay "Vierundsiebzig" (Seventy-four) on the 2014 Yazidi genocide by the Islamic State in Sinjar, Iraq. Othmann co-writes an online column titled "Orient Express" with Cemile Sahin in *taz*, and her personal-political investments are reflected in her other journalistic work as well; she frequently writes about German foreign affairs in the Near East, immigration, discrimination, Kurdish politics, and queerness. The series of poems selected for this issue move with animals in flight, dreams of beds like ships, bittersweet departures, and the body in landscape.

Sharon Dodua Otoo describes herself as "a Black British mother, activist, author and editor." Her parents migrated from Accra, Ghana, to London, England, where she was born and raised. In 1991, Otoo spent a year in Hannover, Germany. Her interest in German came much earlier (ca. 1985) when she started to learn it in school as her second foreign language. After studying German and Management Studies at the University of London, she moved back to Germany, where she resides today, together with her four sons. Since then, she has written numerous literary texts as well as articles for newspapers and journals. She also edits the book series Witnessed and is actively involved with the Initiative Schwarze Menschen in Deutschland (Initiative of Black People in Germany).

Elizabeth Sokol is a PhD student in the Department of Germanic Languages and Literatures at the University of Michigan. Her research interests include early twentieth-century German literature, translation studies, and media studies.

Zafer Şenocak, a German writer born in Ankara in 1961, is the author of a broad and deep oeuvre of poetry, prose, essays, and translations. He writes in German and Turkish. His debut book, the poetry collection *Elektrisches Blau* (*Electrical Blue*, 1983) first established him as a leading contemporary German author and an important voice of bi-culturalism. He has since published numerous novels, essays, translations, and volumes of poetry. His most recent book, *Das Fremde, das in jedem wohnt: Wie Unterschiede unsere Gesellschaft zusammenhalten* (The foreignness that lives in everyone: How differences unite our society, 2018), is an autobiographically inflected reflection on the fear and the abiding value of difference and diversity. He was awarded the Adelbert von Chamisso Prize in 1988. He frequently spends time in the United States at various universities as their writer-in-residence.

Veronica Cook Williamson is a PhD candidate in the Department of Germanic Languages and Literatures at the University of Michigan. Her research interests include post-1989 German literature, the coloniality of migration, modes of translation within and across diasporic Arabic-speaking communities in Germany, and museum studies.

Silke-Maria Weineck is the Grace Lee Boggs Professor of German and Comparative Literature at the University of Michigan. She has been *Absinthe*'s editor-in-chief since the journal moved to the university in 2015.

Serhiy Zhadan is a poet, translator, novelist, and essayist born in Starobilsk, Ukraine. He studied German at Kharkiv University and has been working as a poet, translator, novelist, and essayist since the mid-nineties. His collection of poems, *Warum ich nicht im Netz bin: Gedichte und Prosa aus dem Krieg* (Why I'm not online: Poems and prose from the war), are written from the perspective of the post-independence generation in Ukraine, set during the ongoing Russian occupation and aggression against Ukrainian territories. The collection was first translated to German by Claudia Dathe. Zhadan's poetry showcases the everyday efforts of resistance and solidarity among Ukrainians living on the front lines in eastern Ukraine who seek to uphold their sovereignty and deepen connections with powerful member nations of the European Union rather than Russia. Zhadan participated in numerous pro–European Union protests in Kyiv and has been banned from Russia since 2015.

Source Texts

Alqaseer, Abdullah. "Eine Lüge namens Deutschland." Translated by Mustafa Al-Slaiman. *Weiter Schreiben*. https://weiterschreiben.jetzt/texte/abdullah-alqaseer-eine-luege-namens-deutschland/.

Florescu, Catalin Dorian. "Im Nabel der Welt." In *Swiss Made: Junge Literatur aus der deutschsprachigen Schweiz*, edited by Reto Sorg and Andreas Paschedag, 29–36. Berlin: Verlag Klaus Wagenbach, 2001.

Frenk, Marina. *ewig her und gar nicht wahr*. Berlin: Verlag Klaus Wagenbach, 2020.

Honigmann, Barbara. "Straßburg, 24. Dezember." In *Am Sonntag spielt der Rabbi Fußball: Kleine Prosa*, 5–6. Heidelberg: Wunderhorn, 1998.

Jelinek, Elfriede. "Ballade von drei wichtigen Männern sowie dem Personenkreis um sie herum (Hörspiel)." In *Die endlose Unschuldigkeit: Prosa—Hörspiel—Essay*, 14–48. Schwifting, Germany: Schwiftinger Galerie-Verlag, 1980.

———. *Für den Funk dramatisierte Ballade von drei wichtigen Männern sowie dem Personenkreis um sie herum*, directed by Heinz Hostnig, aired March 27, 1974, NDR/SDR.

———. *Vorspruch zum Hörspiel: "Für den Funk dramatisierte Ballade von drei wichtigen Männern sowie dem Personenkreis um sie herum,"* aired January 14, 1990, SDR.

Neumann, Ronnith. "Begegnung am Meer." In *Ein stürmischer Sonntag: Zornige Geschichten*, 57–62. Berlin: Fischer Taschenbuch Verlag, 1996.

Othmann, Ronya. "[aus dem naturkundemuseum weiß ich]." *Lyrik Line*. https://www.lyrikline.org/en/poems/aus-dem-naturkundemuseum-weiss-ich-14164.

———. "[dass nichts darunter fällt]." *Lyrik Line*. https://www.lyrikline.org/de/gedichte/dass-nichts-darunter-faellt-14155.

———. "[ein in schnee gehetztes reh]." *Lyrik Line*. https://www.lyrikline.org/de/gedichte/ein-schnee-gehetztes-reh-14170.

———. "[es liegt sich auf dünnen laken wie auf papier]." *Lyrik Line*. https://www.lyrikline.org/de/gedichte/es-liegt-sich-auf-duennen-laken-wie-auf-papier-14165.

———. "[wirf die löwenmäulchen hinter dich]." *Lyrik Line*. https://www.lyrikline.org/de/gedichte/wirf-die-loewenmaeulchen-hinter-dich-14154.

Otoo, Sharon Dodua. *Die Geschichte von Kreis und Viereck*. RAA Berlin. 2018. https://raa-berlin.de/wp-content/uploads/2019/01/RAA-BERLIN-DO-DIE-GESCHICHTE-VON-KREIS-UND-VIERECK.pdf.

Şenocak, Zafer. "Vergessene Reisen in die Vergagenheit." Unpublished manuscript, 2020.

———. "Vor Namen." Unpublished manuscript, 2020.

Zhadan, Serhij. *Warum ich nicht im Netz bin: Gedichte und Prosa aus dem Krieg*. Translated by Claudia Dathe. Berlin: Suhrkamp Verlag, 2016.

CPSIA information can be obtained
at www.ICGtesting.com
Printed in the USA
LVHW081618220122
708636LV00011B/171